Brookledge Corporation

7001 Franklin Avenue
Hollywood, California 90028
213-851-3443

Acknowledgements

This book could not have been completed without the seemingly tireless efforts of Bob Busch as well as the help and support from the following wonderful people: Kevin Curtin, Matt and Tori Evans, Hal Hale, Billy McComb, Brian Paradis, Rodney Petreikis, Antonio Ruiz, Bob Sherry, Alison Wolin and Chris Zamiara.

Additional thanks are given to: Paul Butler, Jean Cantor, Shirley Carroll, Eben, Fran and Jim Dale, Don Damaskan, Al Davis, Ernie Evans, Dr. Thomas A. Glover, Geri Larsen Jaffe, Joan Lawton, Peter Pit, John Shrum, Mark Tenfel, Tim Vient and Anne White.

Front Cover: **The Magic Castle**™ at magic hour framed in a 1924 Tiffany gold frame from a desk set belonging to Milt Larsen.

Printed in Canada

Milt Larsen's Magical Mystery Tour of Hollywood's Most Amazing Landmark

The Magic Castle™

Written & Photographed
By
Carol Marie

Based on Milt Larsen's
personal tours

Contents

There is a mysterious structure perched on a hillside in Holly-wood, California. It looks something like the artwork that flowed from the pen of the ghoulish cartoonist, Charles Addams. This is the landmark home which is now known as The Magic Castle. Over the past three decades the 5,000 members of the Academy of Magical Arts have called it "home."

Foreward

Over the years people have often asked about the history of the building and the curious collections that may be found within the magical walls of the old house. To answer those questions I started giving monthly walking tours of the Castle for those who were interested. The tours were usually limited to about twenty people — that was, of course, twenty people plus Carol Marie.

Carol Marie followed me through the Castle making copious notes, asking questions, taking pictures and audio taping the sessions. This book is the result of her efforts. This is not a book about the magicians of the Academy of Magical Arts or even of the Magic Castle itself. This is simply a book for members and guests who have visited the club over the years and would like to know more about it. There are hundreds of pictures of the Magic Castle, and, of course, for many of these pictures there is a story or an anecdote that accompanies it ... but that will be another book in the future.

Please be aware that this book may be filled with many errors and omissions. Carol Marie has done a meticulous job of gathering all the information and double checking the historical facts. On the other hand I have driven her crazy because the Magic Castle is constantly changing. Not just changing by hanging a new painting here and there or moving some furniture; we have been known to change entire rooms overnight! Part of the charm of the Castle is that it is constantly fresh and exciting.

For me, the Magic Castle will never be finished and, as long as other old buildings keep getting torn down, and as long as people keep cleaning out their attics, we'll keep adding to **THE MAGIC CASTLE.**

Please enjoy your walking tour of the club. Keep your arms and elbows in the boat and please don't feed the crocodiles!

Milt Larsen

7

The Lane Mansion

The beautiful Victorian mansion, which is now the Magic Castle was originally a private home built in 1908 by a banker and real estate magnate, Rollin B. Lane. Mr. Lane owned much of what is now Hollywood. He had seen a beautiful French "Chateau" or Gothic Renaissance-style Victorian home in Redlands, California. That house was built in 1897 and was purchased by the Kimberly family in 1905. Kimberly Crest, designed by Dennis & Farwell, was a two-story, seventeen room house that included four bedrooms, library/sitting room, music room, dining room, servant's quarters/steamer trunk storage area, parlour, an orchestra mezzanine, five bathrooms, a large basement, and a finished attic. Mr. Lane hired the same contractors who built the Kimberly Crest to recreate a duplicate on the hillside in Hollywood. Mr. Lane made only one change in the original plan. He wanted the impressive four story high tower to dominate the corner of the house facing Los Angeles. The result is the Lane mansion has the appearance of a mirror image of Kimberly Crest.

Kimberly Crest

1906 view of Orchid Avenue

In 1905 a theatrical guide described Hollywood as a "railroad depot five miles from Los Angeles." But Mr. Lane recognized Hollywood as a rich agricultural area; a great location for farms and ranches. When Mr. Lane purchased his property, he envisioned a grand home overlooking his future orange groves. He thought it would be an excellent business investment. The orchard was to span the area from the Lane mansion south to the street north of Hollywood High School called Lanewood Lane.

1907 view looking south from Franklin

Unfortunately, the dream of orange blossoms faded away with the drought of 1905. By the time Mr. Lane moved his family into his new home in 1908, the parched ranch lands had failed. Orange Drive was, then, simply a road through the center of what was Mr. Lane's orange grove. And Hollywood had become a desert doomed to a future of commercial and residential real estate development.

Over the years the Lane home was one of several mansions that created an exclusive neighborhood in Hollywood, with such owners as Sid Grauman (owner of the Grauman Theater chain which included Hollywood's Grauman's Chinese), L. Frank Baum (author of "The Wizard of Oz"), producers Sam Goldwyn and Mack Sennett, and celebrities like Errol Flynn, Janet Gaynor, Russ Colombo, William Faulkner and Jean Harlow. Mr. Lane was a good friend of producer Jesse Lasky and may have helped in the financing of the Lasky/DeMille film "The Squaw Man" which is credited with bringing the film industry to Hollywood.

The Lane family lived in the mansion until the early 1940's. Following their departure, the house was divided into a duplex-style, multifamily home. For a short time after that, the house was used as a home for the elderly and in the 1950's, it was again divided into even smaller apartments. Tenants painted the natural wood paneling and false walls that subdivided the house into a maze of small living quarters. While the deterioration of the inside of the house was occurring, the natural elements took a heavy toll on the exterior of the building. And by 1960, the once proud Victorian house was in such a state of disrepair that it was in danger of being demolished.

Lane Mansion 1962

Milt Larsen was a writer on the NBC TV show "Truth or Consequences" starring Bob Barker. Many a day he would view a rather tattered-and-torn house surrounded by weed-filled grounds from his 9th floor Ralph Edwards Productions office at Highland Avenue and Hollywood Boulevard. The house in the overgrown garden was the Lane mansion. Remembering his father's lifelong dream of an elegant private magician's club, Milt envisioned that house as a realization of his father's dream.

Milt arranged to meet the imposing Texan, Thomas Glover Sr., who owned the land now occupied by the Yamashiro Restaurant, the Magic Castle, the Magic Hotel and the apartments in-between. During the meeting, Milt revealed his mechanical technology of a disappearing Cinemascope screen at Larsen family home in Los Angeles. Milt traded his technology that would enable Tom Glover to open the heavy plate-glass windows at the Yamashiro and the promise of providing similar miracles in restoring the Lane mansion for the opportunity to convert the house into the elegant private magician's club of his father's dreams.

Milt persevered. He convinced the owner that the house was a potential example of the elegance that was once Hollywood and approximately one year later, September 1961, Mr. Thomas O. Glover extended his hand in a legendary Texas handshake that was the beginning of the Magic Castle. Milt and Tom had finally reached an agreement to begin renovations.

Milt's brother Bill Larsen Jr., took on the enormous task of organizing a new nonprofit California Corporation, the Academy of Magical Arts. Bill was a cost-control executive and associate producer at CBS TV at that time. Milt operated a typewriter and a hammer but it was Bill who knew how to run an adding machine. Bill was designated to handle the business and administrative side of the club and Milt's mission was to create a physical castle of magic. For the next year, Milt, early partner Don Gotschall, and their friends spent endless hours of spare time and countless gallons of paint remover while they stripped layers of white paint from the carved wood paneling, detailed fireplace mantels, and stained glass windows. It was during this renovation that Milt invited John Shrum, a friend and NBC art director of "Truth or Consequences" to view the challenge. With a love for Victorian architecture, John Shrum instantly, upon viewing the mansion, agreed to become the artistic designer for the restoration of the old Lane home.

Shortly after Milt began scraping paint off woodwork in the Lane mansion, he found another old house: The Waters mansion at the corner of Portland Avenue and Adams, or 900 W. Adams, to be precise. In 1961, the destruction of magnificent homes from "Millionaires Row" had begun to make way for more commercial apartment houses. Built in 1888, the Waters mansion was a Victorian delight but had unfortunately become the victim of cruel vandalism. Milt located the wrecking company, and then negotiated and purchased the contents of the condemned house for the amount of its address: 900 dollars!

year and three months later, with thousands of man hours, gallons of paint remover, hundreds of board feet of rescued antique paneling, and dozens of stunning art glass windows, the dream had become a reality. The big moment had arrived.

n January 2, 1963, the Magic Castle was slated to open its doors. In those days, the physical license was necessary to purchase the liquor. Due to the holiday, the liquor license was not official until January 2nd and the liquor distributor had to wait for an approval from Sacramento before any alcohol could be purchased. The physical document did not reach Milt's hands until 4 p.m. opening day. But fortunately, a founding Member, Snag Werris, provided the truck to haul the liquor to the Magic Castle. He arrived at 5 p.m. to save the day!

he paint had not dried in the ladies room so a sign was hung on the men's room door reading: "Tonight only - Boys and Girls." The ever proper John Shrum placed a beautiful bouquet of flowers in the urinal and the mansion opened its doors (by the skin of its teeth) as the Magic Castle precisely at 6 p.m. Mark Wilson stood on Irma's piano and floated Nani (a photo of which appeared in Newsweek Magazine) and Bill and Irene welcomed guests while the incomparable Jay Ose entertained them.

1/14/63 Newsweek-Mark & Nani Wilson

The Magic Castle was a hit! The partnership of the Victorian architecture coupled with the incredible talents of the club's members led to the success of this magical and entertaining establishment.

The Magic Castle 1963

Even as guests partied in three rooms on the main floor, Milt Larsen and his friends continued their restoration of other areas. In October of 1963, the first dining room opened to guests and, room by room, the Magic Castle continued to grow. In 1966, the William Larsen, Sr. Memorial Library was opened in the third floor servant's quarters area, shortly followed by the Haunted Wine Cellar in the basement.

1976 construction

By 1974, however, the popularity of the clubhouse had grown to the point that the building could not legally hold the number of people who were appearing at the front door every evening. At that time, the main showroom for the stage magicians was what is now the Museum in the Haunted Wine Cellar. Because it seated approximately fifty people, it was totally inadequate for the nightly guests often numbering two hundred. In addition, since the stage ceiling height was only seven feet, it could not accommodate large illusions or tall magicians.

Shimada, a wonderful magician from Japan, performed in the theatre. But he kept forgetting the ceiling was only seven feet tall. He had one particular illusion that used flaming umbrellas. Unfortunately, Milt was not the only one concerned with Shimada's flaming umbrellas; the fire department worried as well. After digging in the files, the only permit that could be found for the Magic Castle was issued in 1962 and was hardly adequate to cover the increasing occupancy over the years.

Shimada 1974

After warning the club several times, the fire inspector ended his leniency. On a surprise inspection, the fire inspector insisted on either sprinklers or an occupancy of fifty people. A party of 200 attorneys had been booked for that very night! The Larsens tried to pull strings. They called everyone they knew to promise, cajole, beg - anything to not have to cancel the party. The fire department, backed by City Hall, was adamant and would not budge. The only concession the fire department was willing to make was to allow the party to take place in the parking structure of the Magic Castle.

The major problem was that the parking structure looked like a concrete, steel-reinforced bomb shelter underground parking garage.

Garage structure 1975

At 3 p.m. Milt broke the unpardonable rule of not calling John Shrum during a "Tonight Show" production meeting. But this was an emergency! The Magic Castle had three hours to convert the parking structure into a party room for 200 ready-to-sue lawyers! John started the wagons rolling. Trucks started arriving from NBC, Paramount, Universal, Walter Allen Plant Rental and, by 6 p.m., the parking structure had been turned into an incredibly beautiful night club with three practical bars. Marvyn Roy (a.k.a. Mr. Electric) performed that night in the parking lot theatre. For the next thirty days the Magic Castle operated out of that temporary night club while fire sprinklers were being installed in the main building. But an idea had been born.

Mr. Electric

Marvyn Roy, parking lot theatre

nce again, in spite of the gigantic risk involved, Milt received permission from both the Board of Directors and owner Thomas Glover to proceed with the building of two new theaters utilizing the center level of the three-story parking garage, built into the hillside west of the house. This could only be accomplished by the Glovers building a completely new two story service building between the two existing structures. The structure was named the Thomas O. Glover Theater Annex. This new wing, which opened in June of 1976, included a theater designed for parlour-style magic and a full theater of 130 seats with a stage that accommodated large illusions. John Shrum, once again, provided his talents and expertise in creating the decor of the addition, imperceptibly blending it into the 1908 design so that guests never realize they are stepping out of the original mansion.

n 1989, the Los Angeles Cultural Heritage Commission voted to place the Magic Castle on the list of Los Angeles Cultural Heritage Monuments as #406. The landmark status actually refers to the old Lane mansion that is buried somewhere beneath all the antique bric-a-brac that decorates it. It has won many awards and has been lauded for its "imaginative constructive reuse of an historical building."

The house that Milt built, as Bill Larsen described it in an issue of Genii Magazine, is a museum of old buildings intricately scattered throughout the old Victorian home. With the help of Ernie Evans (the man with the velvet crowbar who had a rare talent for finding and saving architectural treasures from houses and buildings that were being destroyed from Long Beach to San Francisco) Milt and John Shrum took a little here, put it there. Here a little, there a little and Viola!: **The Magic Castle.**

When Rollin B. Lane built a house for his family at the beginning of this century, he could not have known that it would become one of the most famous and recognizable mansions in the world, and home to many of the greatest magicians and celebrities of today.

Thomas O. Glover, Sr.

The late Thomas O. Glover, Sr. was a visionary. He came to Hollywood shortly after World War II and saw the real estate potential of the area through the eyes of a banker and real estate developer. Tom was from Texas and was educated at Standard University. He loved football and was an accomplished musician, playing many musical instruments.

In the late 1950's, Tom purchased much of the ten acres of land that includes what is now the Magic Castle, the Yamashiro restaurant and apartments, the Magic Hotel and several other apartment buildings. He created the family organization that still watches over the Glover interests on the hill, now headed by his wife, Lucille Glover, and managed by his son, Dr. Thomas A. Glover. Mr. Glover also had a great interest in civic affairs and was responsible for a number of engineering and traffic improvements in the community.

When Milt Larsen met Tom Glover in 1961, it was the meeting of a dreamer and a businessman with certain dreams of his own. Tom Glover was one of the greatest fans of the Magic Castle and always considered it one of his most cherished accomplishments.

Front Entrance/Fountain

When the turreted Lane mansion on the knoll overlooking fields of potential orange groves was finished in 1908, the front door and porch faced south. A circular walkway curled around a large lawn and rose garden that filled the property all the way to Franklin. Since that time, restoration and additions to both the original house and the neighborhood have changed its appearance.

As you turn into the driveway at 7001 Franklin Avenue, you are on part of the original circular walkway that enclosed the large rose garden. The entrance to the house was moved to the east side to accommodate a parking structure to the west and a new road to Yamashiro in 1964. Guests frequently comment on how small the Magic Castle appears when seen from the outside but how large it seems once they start to explore the interior. Could it be that the house magically grows in size once you enter it? This book will take you on a tour through the Magic Castle floor by floor, room by room, showing you how it developed into the showplace of the magic world. The Magic Castle is known to magicians and an international public as the premier magic institution and the Headquarters of Magic.

The friendly valet service greets all visitors to the Magic Castle. As you exit your vehicle, note the view of Hollywood between the statuesque Cypress and Hollywood palm trees of the driveway. Two lions are sentinels to the Magic Castle entrance, symbols of the regal splendor waiting beyond the entrance doors.

The Lion motif fountain (A1) with the stoic lions on either side of the pond came from a grand apartment in the Alvarado district where William Desmond Taylor, the Quixotic film director, was murdered (most likely by Edward F. Sands on February 1, 1922). No one was ever prosecuted in this notorious scandal that included typical Hollywood rumors about a young, beautiful actress. Perhaps the stone lions know the secret.

Behind the lion fountain are two iron light standards (A2) that were recovered from an old library in Riverside.

The ornate three-globe lamps (A3) that border the front of the house were street lights in Philadelphia circa 1900's.

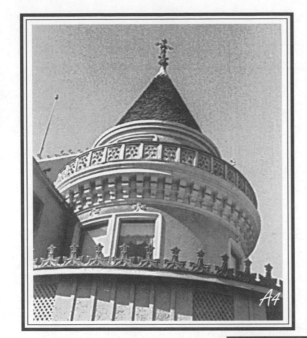

The roof cresting decorations are pressed zinc (A4) and border the entire roof line. More were added as the second story porch was enclosed in 1974. They were cast from the original 1900's patterns.

The grand Ionic capitals (A5) originally ornamented the arches of the colonnades at Venice Pier, California, as part of Abbot Kinney's vision to create a Venetian utopia in America.

The large canopy (A6) over the front entrance was an addition in 1965. The cast iron frieze work and the canopy were part of the entrance to a Lodge at Wilshire and LaBrea. The addition of the canopy was adventuresome and not without major mishap. Catch Milt one day when you have a few hours and ask him how easy it was to install...

This staff-plaster ornamental gable (A7) was one of the original gables of the Lane mansion and is indicative of elegant Victorian homes at the turn-of-the-century. Two carved lions support a herald of England. These gables were identical to those in Kimberly Crest, although Kimberly Crest's gables have subsequently been covered and are no longer visible.

The mansard roof (A8) of the iron frieze canopy was added later incorporating an art glass window from a church. The original crucifix was replaced with the Magic Castle initials and installed behind the owl, a symbol of the Magic Castle.

Reception/Entry Hall

Once the library and sitting room of the Lane Mansion, the Entry Hall sets the magical theme of the Magic Castle. Notice there is only one door - the one from which you entered!

Near the turn-of-the-century, a number of mansions were built along Adams Boulevard near downtown Los Angeles. This residential section was nicknamed "Millionaires Row." In the early 1960's these stately homes were slowly being demolished as freeways cut through some of Los Angeles' finest old residential areas. At one such home, the Waters mansion at Adams and Portland, Milt arranged to remove all the fixtures, mahogany woodwork and decorative windows prior to the wrecking crew's arrival. Although pieces from the 1888 Waters mansion can be found in nearly every room of the Magic Castle, the Entry Hall is a fine example of the quality woodwork and stained glass treasures that were saved from destruction.

Passing through the ornate double doors, you will find yourself stepping back in time. The Victorian ambiance is reflected in the rich woodwork, ceiling paintings and furnishings that fill each room of the house. The reception area was originally the library in the Lane mansion and the entrance doorway was once a large bay window.

Originally the street address for the Lane mansion was 701 Franklin Avenue. However, as the Los Angeles area grew and developed, the street numbering also increased. Eventually, the address became 7001 Franklin Avenue as it is today.

Reception area 1963

As additions and renovations occurred throughout the years, several showcases were designed to offer Magic Castle memorabilia and mementos. Feel free to browse. The receptionist will confirm your dinner reservations, verify that you are over 21 and that you are dressed properly for the evening. Next you will receive the evening's theatrical schedule and be directed to the Phantom's Knight and the Open Sesame Owl. But before you venture out of this room, take a moment to look around.

B1

The overhead chandelier (B1) belonged to Nellie Bean (wife of the Hanging Judge Roy Bean) and came from their home in Pocatello, Idaho. It is one of the first chandeliers designed to accommodate both gas and electricity that provided illumination no matter what the emergency. The electric lights point down while the gas lamps face upwards. It is interesting to note that the entire Lane home was "plumbed" for both gas lights and electricity.

The red-flocked wallpaper (B2) was chosen by Milt Larsen. John Shrum cringed politely when he saw it. During the fifties and sixties, every Gay '90's, Roaring '20's bar was decorated with red-flocked wallpaper. Milt promised John the flocked wallpaper would never be changed as it was a tribute to Milt's bad taste. From then on, Milt always contacted John prior to redecorating.

B3/B4

━✦━ The richly carved oak fireplace (B3) is the original mantel from the Lane mansion. Milt's wife, Arlene, found the brass fireplace in London.

━✦━ The large black and white photo (B4) above the fireplace is an aerial view of the Lane mansion circa 1924. Billy McComb dated the photograph by the age of the cars present, while Milt merely looked at the back of the photo where the date was prominent. At the bottom of the photograph is Hollywood Boulevard and the future locations of the famous Grauman's Chinese Theater and the Roosevelt Hotel. On the hill above the Lane mansion is the Bernheimer Estate, now the Yamashiro Restaurant.

B5

The front doors (B5) came from the Waters mansion as well as the paneling and woodwork. The cut glass windows were replaced with leaded crystal by Hiram Strait, (a.k.a. Jeffrey Kessler), member of the Magic Castle. Hiram designed the Magic Castle's initials as an integral part of the windows: MC. He also incorporated a fault in each door section as "only the Almighty is perfect."

B6

The art glass window (B6) behind the receptionists' desk was once a prominent window from a home in England. Moved just prior to this printing, the window now resides as the west wall of the Terrace Dining Room.

B7

✦✦✦ Manufactured by Richard Diamond Productions in conjunction with Lynn West Designs, Richard, in the form of an holographic effect, (B7) offers a Phantom Knight's welcome to the Magic Castle.

B8

The Open Sesame Owl (B8), with its red blinking eyes, controls the passage to the Grand Salon. The gilded carved owl (who serves as the guardian of this mysterious mansion) was part of a piece of furniture that belonged to the Larsen family dating back to the turn-of-the-century. The Open Sesame Owl gained amazing powers once given a permanent home at the Magic Castle.

nly by whispering the phrase that opened a world of wonder to Aladdin in his famed 1,001 nights, "OPEN SESAME" will the carved mysterious owl open the bookcase to reveal a secret passageway into the Grand Salon, amidst a crash of thunder and a flash of lightning.

Along the passageway to the Grand Salon is a framed enlargement of a 1920's postcard (B9) of the Bernheimer Gardens: A Japanese Bungalow. The Bernheimer Gardens was built in 1911 and is now known as the Yamashiro Restaurant. Apartments surround the garden/pond area and ring the hillside. It is owned and operated by the Glover family and offers Los Angeles' most spectacular view of the city.

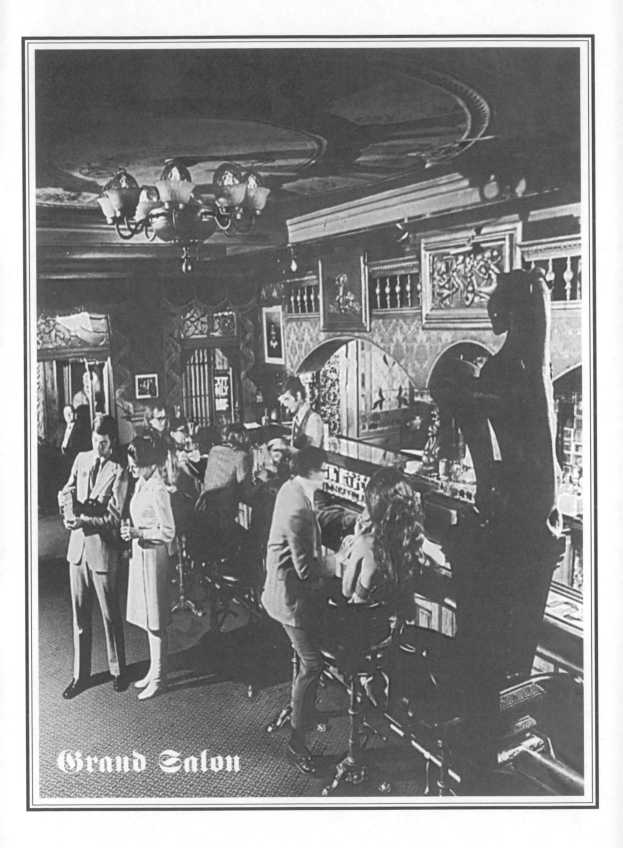

Grand Salon

Once the Grand Hall of the Lane Mansion, this magnificent room serves as the central meeting room for the Magic Castle, the apex of activity. From this room you have access to all the mysteries and wonderment that can be found at the Magic Castle.

As you face the Grand Salon bar, to the right, the Gothic Stairway leads upstairs to four dining rooms, the Houdini Seance Room, the Palace of Mystery Theater, the Palace Bar and Lounge, the Parlour of Prestidigitation, the Inner Circle, the Albert Peller Theater and the William W. Larsen Memorial Library. To the left is the Blackstone Room, Invisible Irma's Room, the Hat & Hare Pub, the Museum in the Haunted Wine Cellar, and the Close-Up Gallery. So many choices! But we will begin right here, at the Grand Salon bar.

In 1963, when the Magic Castle first opened, the Grand Salon bar only extended to half of what it is now, or up to the exit door of the old dining room. It was extended to its present length during one of Milt's numerous renovations. In the early days, the Magic Castle was closed for two weeks every year to allow Milt the ability to make renovations that would have inhibited business. As a result, the Magic Castle grew, displays changed rooms, rooms changed locations and even though the Magic Castle is no longer closed for two weeks a year, Milt still changes everything whenever he can!

C1/C2

⟡ Two red velvet settees and marble table (C1) comprise an area reserved exclusively for the legendary "Professor" Dai Vernon (1894-1992) when he was in the club. Dai spent hours here with fellow magicians as well as entertained nightly guests with his unique style of close-up magic.

⟡ The portrait (C2) of the Ancient Mariner, behind the settee, is an ancestral family member of the Larsens from Norway. Unfortunately he had no particular magical talents of his own but his presence is undeniable and omniscient.

Out of the 170+ art glass windows currently in the Magic Castle, the three leaded crystal windows (C3) that encompass the doorway on the south wall and lead into the Blackstone Room are the only remaining original ornate windows from the Lane mansion.

Paneling from the rescued Waters mansion fronts the large Grand Salon bar (C4) while the top comes from the ballroom floor of the same mansion. The parquet bar top is made of hundreds of hand-tooled pieces of eight different types of hard woods.

C5/C7

C6

◄✖✖✖ A large Bavarian beer pump (C5) from the early 1800's resides beneath the center arch of the Grand Salon bar. The sculpted portion depicts Gambrinus; a Flemish King of mythology who, according to legend, was the creator of beer.

◄✖✖✖ The well-endowed winged beasts (C6) that support the arches for the bar were once legs of a library table. This more visible location brings their carved attributes to light for us.

◄✖✖✖ The glass beaded lace (C7) decorating the bar is the type found on the finest Tiffany lamps of the turn-of-the-century. It was selected because it matches the glass lace depicted in the very rare lithograph of Chung Ling Soo at the end of the bar.

The theatre lantern slides (C8) came from the Hippodrome Theatre in Los Angeles. They were once used to advertise coming attractions and performers scheduled to appear at the popular Vaudeville theatre circa 1916-1920's. News of the Hippodrome's pending demolition in the early 1950's had reached Milt. Wanting to see the theatre prior to its demise, Milt paid a quarter to visit the then sleazy 24-hour "flop house" cinema where you could be left alone all night for two bits. Because of his interest in the old building, Milt was given a personal tour and, literally, stumbled over a box of old lantern slides, which was graciously offered to him. Milt's entire lantern slide collection cost 25¢!

The bas relief sculpture "Sweet Charity" above the Grand Salon bar (C9) is one of the Three Grace sculptures (Faith, Hope & Charity) made for William Randolph Hearst for his San Simeon "castle." Originally it resided in Phoebe Hearst's bedroom. "Sweet Charity" was donated to the Magic Castle by Member Hubert Sommers in 1966. Executed by famed artist Olin Leviwarner (1844-1896), this single piece of art was appraised in 1966 for $2,500.

44

The Victorian alabaster and bronze chandelier (C10) is suspended from the pivotal apex of the uniquely painted ceiling. Painted by NBC artist, Jim Dodson, the ceiling (C11) above the Grand Salon bar reflects the tumultuous skies of Dante's Inferno.

Added later is a devilish caricature of Milt Larsen (C12) as he peers through the ceiling to keep an eye on the bartenders.

C13

◄CMMK The black and white etched-style portraits of President and Mrs. Andrew Jackson (C13) gaze out from either side of the Grand Salon bar. They are another addition by the talented scenic artists of NBC.

◄CMMK The Atwater Kent radio (C14) allows you to reminisce about the old radio shows of yesteryear. Pick up the earphones and you may hear the trapped sounds of "The Lone Ranger" or "Fibber McGee and Molly." Many times impromptu props were "stashed" away inside the radio by magicians, not knowing the radio a practical prop. This caused many hours of frustration until Milt finally figured out why the radio needed constant repair.

C14

C 15

One of five rare Chung Ling Soo posters (C15) repeats the Victorian beaded lace effect that decorates the bar. The four additional Chung Ling Soo posters are in the Palace of Mystery bar area and represent a very limited edition, original artwork effort on the part of art students in the communities where Chung Ling Soo performed.

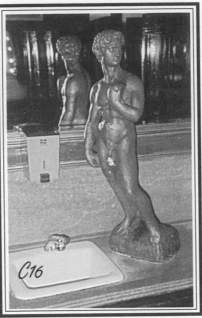

C16

On the east side of the Gothic Staircase you will find the "rooms of convenience" in which Milt's decorative touches can be found. In the ladies bathroom there is a moderately obscene statue of David (C16) that dispenses soap.

In the men's bathroom, immediately left of the door is the Great Alibi machine (C17), situated by the pay telephone. The vintage control box provides background sound effects to corroborate that phony story you are telling your boss or wife about your current whereabouts.

C17

C18

The Shane's Castle (C18) in Ireland, incorporates iridescent butterfly wings as accents to the castle. Member Billy McComb swears he was born behind the twin peaks, on the road to Belfast, and that his brother's ashes were scattered in that very Lough (Lake) Neagh.

Sorcar (1913-1971) from Bengali, India was a famed stage illusionist. He billed himself as the World's Greatest Magician and was noted for his elaborate performances, costumes and publicity. His oil portrait (C19) hangs to the left of the exit and was painted by Salvatore Salla. In 1956 on the BBC, the Television Panorama Show of Sorcar's illusion ran too long and the climax to his "Sawing the Woman in Half" was not culminated on air. The station was deluged with thousands of phone calls from people concerned about the separated woman.

C19

C20

The oil portrait by Salvatore Salla of the Oriental Magician (C20) above the original fireplace depicts Dutch Wizard Theo Bamberg (1875-1963), disguised as his alter ego "Okito," performing his famed illusion "The Floating Sphere." Occidental magicians usually did not differentiate between the Asian cultures, thus the Japanese named Okito wears a Chinese costume. "Okito" is an anagram of Kioto where the Mikado held his court. Theo's son, David Bamberg's (1904-1974) alter ego was "Fu-Manchu." David represents the seventh generation of magicians from the Bamberg family.

Grand Salon prior to renovation

Grand Salon construction 1965

Grand Salon in 1963.

The Magic Castle has its own breed of special drinks, including the likes of: Houdini's Escape, Irma's Sonata, Castle Coffee Mephisto, Gray Ghost, The Count's Cooler, Hare's Breath, Magic Toad Martini and The Creaky Castle. All of our bartenders are well versed in these specials and would be more than happy to accommodate your requests here at the Grand Salon bar.

WARNING! Visitors to the Magic Castle must be careful at all times. Many guests have reported walls that keep an eye on them. Others have seen portraits that follow them as they pass through the rooms; that tables have mysteriously moved and bar stools have imperceptibly shrunk in size while someone was seated in them. Nothing is impossible at the Magic Castle! But you HAVE been warned!

The Magic Castle is the only private club in the world that has successfully featured magical entertainment for over thirty years. Presenting seven or more different magicians a week in three showrooms, the Magic Castle is one of the most popular gathering places for some of Hollywood's biggest celebrities.

For more than a quarter of a century, the Magic Castle has taken pride in the quality of performers who have appeared in its showrooms. One of its earliest performers here at the Magic Castle was Harry Blackstone, Sr. He delighted in levitating pretty ladies, such as Irene Larsen, and used the area in the Grand Salon as his impromptu theatre.

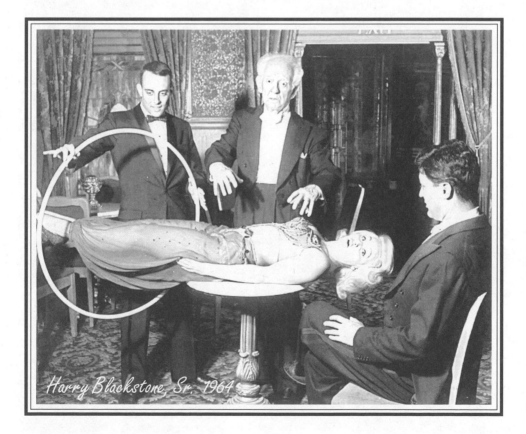

Harry Blackstone, Sr. 1964

As you leave the Grand Salon area and enter the Blackstone Room, on your left, observe the marquee that announces the artists that will be performing in all of the showrooms for the evening.

The Blackstone Room

The Blackstone Room was once the grand outdoor veranda of the Lane mansion. When the road to the top of the hill was completed in 1964, this room was enclosed and the entrance to the Magic Castle was moved to the east. This room is dedicated to The Blackstones. To multiple generations of Americans, the Blackstone name meant the finest spectacular presentations of magic and illusions of all time.

Harry Blackstone, Sr. started it all near the beginning of the 20th century. Harry Sr. lived down the street from the Magic Castle on Sycamore Avenue and frequented the establishment often where demonstrations of his closeup magic still baffled and amazed our early guests who were always pleasantly surprised to find one of the most legendary names in the history of magic entertaining in the Blackstone Room.

Harry, Jr. carried on his father's name and constantly added luster to the art of magic. His stage show was a full magic extravaganza reminiscent of the bygone days of vaudeville.

D1

A larger-than-life sized bust (D1) of Harry Blackstone (1885-1965) was donated in 1963, ten years after the artist, James V. Gentilly passed away. Dr. Gentilly was a famous dentist from Cleveland, Ohio. He was a teacher, essayist, clinician, humanitarian,sculptor, painter, artist, editor, magician and personal friend of Harry Blackstone.

~◆✕✕✕< The beautiful mahogany woodwork (D2) and stained glass windows (D3) were once originally part of the Odd Fellow's Lodge in Los Angeles and provide the framed arch for the Blackstone bust.

~◆✕✕✕< The artwork in the room consists of different artists conceptions of the great magician. The oil portrait of Blackstone with three doves (D4) was painted by an NBC scenic artist.

~◆✕✕✕< One of the small portraits (D5) of Harry Blackstone, facing front, was painted by Mickey O'Malley. The side view portrait is a color photograph (D6) on canvas.

The Blackstone poster (D7) on display is an original lithograph from 1920 and depicts the phenomenal "Oriental Nights" production extravaganza from the Blackstone touring show. Included in the production was the vanish of the Enchanted Camel and the Phantom Stallion, a Cannon Illusion and the famous Indian Rope Trick surrounded by the regal splendor of Solomon's Court. Blackstone ceased touring in the 1950's.

Harry Blackstone (1885-1965)

Born Harry Boughton, the young magician began his career working the vaudeville circuits with his brother, Pete. He performed as Henri Bouton, then Fredrick, the Great. Finally, on the advice of agents, he changed his name to Blackstone during World War I, naming himself after a popular hotel in Chicago. (Billy McComb credits the name change to a billboard advertising Blackstone cigars that Harry viewed from his hotel room).

By 1925 Blackstone was a recognized name in the world of magic. Unlike his chief competitor, Howard Thurston, who was known for his dramatic presentations, Blackstone was noted for his casual, friendly style of performing.

Blackstone's magical repertoire included a wide variety of illusions, from the terrifying penetration of a buzz saw through an assistant's body to the amazing vanish of a bird cage from his fingertips while completely surrounded by the audience. He was known internationally as a performer and was worshipped by children as a super hero. His life was serialized in "Blackstone Master Magician" comic books and the Blackstone radio show.

He was, in addition, a magical pioneer in the world of television and appeared on such programs as "The Jackie Gleason Show," Edward R. Murrow's "Face To Face" and "This Is Your Life."

Following his retirement, Harry Blackstone moved to Southern California for health reasons. He made one of his final stage appearances on Milt Larsen's "It's Magic!" show in 1960. Paying tribute to the timeless greatness of the celebrated conjurer, "The New Tops," a magician's magazine wrote: Harry Blackstone, occupation: legend.

⚡ Harry Blackstone, Jr. (D8) utilized, in several instances, the original equipment and props that Harry, Sr. developed and constructed. One of their most famous effects was "The Floating Lightbulb." Harry developed the art of magic into something both unique and arrestingly modern, reverent of the past but injecting an innovative presentation of the future.

Harry Blackstone Jr (1934-1997)

Harry Blackstone, Jr. was born in Three Rivers, Michigan in 1934 as the only child of Harry Sr. and Billie Matthews. Even though Harry began performing in his father's show at the tender age of six months, he didn't graduate to mental telepathy until he was four. At the age of seven, Harry Jr. began to tour with his father.

Schooled by his father in the aspects of magic, illusion and showmanship, Harry Jr. brilliantly continued the Blackstone legend for new generations of audiences.

In 1974, Harry Jr. married his principal assistant, Gay Blevins, a former Golddigger dancer on the Dean Martin Show. Together they worked the Playboy Club circuit followed by appearances in Las Vegas and on various TV venues: The Tonight Show, Merv Griffin, Michael Douglas, Dinah Shore, and subsequently on a magic special. Harry Jr.'s full-length show, that recreated his father's most celebrated illusions, toured throughout United States and included an 118 night run on Broadway, making Harry Jr. the longest running illusionist/magician to perform in the history of New York theatre.

Harry Jr. was named Magician of the Year in 1979 and again in 1985 and received the Academy of Magical Arts' highest award, the Master Fellowship Award in 1994. In 1985 he co-authored "The Blackstone Book of Magic and Illusion." In 1990 the Blackstones appeared in "The Blackstone Family TV Special" in Japan. Vintage film footage of Harry Sr. combined with live performances by Harry Jr. and his youngest daughter, Bellamine, marked an historic event as it was the first time three generations of Blackstones appeared together on the same stage. Harry Jr. was an avid supporter of the Magic Castle and served on the Board of Directors as Vice-President until his unexpected death in 1997.

o the right and the left of the Blackstone Room are two staircases that lead into what was once the basement of the Lane mansion. The Hat & Hare Pub and Museum in the Haunted Wine Cellar are downstairs. However, due to the proximity, we will next venture into Irma's Room, which is to the right.

Irma's Room as the Close Up Gallery 1963

Invisible Irma's Room

nce the dining room of the Lane mansion, this room was the first Close-Up Gallery before being converted into Irma's music room. Jay Ose, Resident Magician and first host of the Magic Castle, performed intimate close-up magic here in the club's first year.

rma™ became a house guest ghost when the Lanes resided here and she loved playing the piano. She was relegated to the attic during the deterioration of the house after the Lanes moved. However, legend has it, when the Lane mansion became the Magic Castle in 1963, Irma's piano was found in the attic. The piano was dusted off, tuned up, and moved back into the main portion of the house. Luckily for us, Irma, and Katy, followed.

Irma's canary, Katy, is Irma's constant companion. She will occasionally respond to enthusiastic guests who show their generosity and appreciation by placing greenbacks in her cage.

Irma has an unquenchable thirst and will gratefully accept libations HOWEVER she is limited in the quantity of drinks in one night. The cocktail waitress keeps strict tabs on her quota.

In the old days of the Magic Castle, Invisible Irma was frequently visited by her brother, Invisible Irving (who was quite a distinguished tap dancer) and Invisible Isabella (a topless dancer living in San Francisco). Invisible Isabella would oft times accompany Irma with her drums (of course, topless).

Irma is a happy ghost, always adding her delightful sense of humor to any question you may ask. And even though she passed away in 1932, her musical talents include a current repertoire of melodies as well as those from her own era. She loves to play your requests.

The Baldwin grand piano (E1), originally owned by Jose Iturbi, (a famed classical concert pianist who appeared in many MGM musicals) is the fourth and finest piano that Irma has played on at the Magic Castle. Irma performs nightly, Friday lunches and Sunday brunches.

E2

One of the portraits in this chamber is Irma as a child. Ernie Evans, from Scavenger's Paradise, had found an antique grand gold frame that needed a home. Obscured by dust, it was impossible to see the portrait. When Milt cleaned the painting, he exposed a charming Victorian pastel (E2) of a naked child sitting in a chair. When it was hung in the Irma room, Irma immediately played "Yes Sir, That's My Baby" so Milt assumed it must have been an early painting of the ghost. To this day, this portrait hangs in Irma's Room as a remembrance of her early days in Chicago.

The exquisite lady adorning the ceiling (E3) was painted by NBC scenic artist, Bill McGuire. It is a reproduction of a postcard illustration by Czechoslovakian Art Nouveau artist, Alphonse Maria Mucha (1860-1939) entitled "Daydream" 1896. The bronze and crystal chandelier is one of the few remaining original Lane Mansion chandeliers.

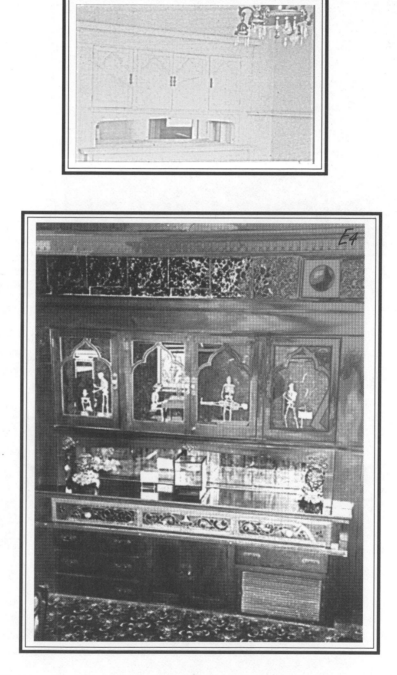

~~~ The carved mahogany china buffet (E4) is original to the Lane mansion as are the fireplace mantel and paneling. Unfortunately they were all covered in a thick salt-and-pepper "Zolotone" paint which had to be painstakingly re-moved to restore them to their present condition of splendor.

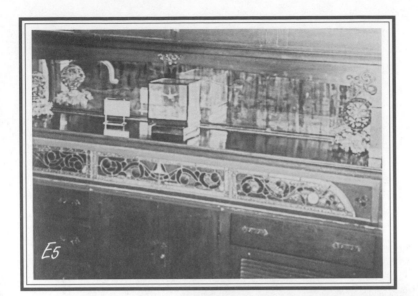

The art glass pieces (E5) that face the buffet are from the Waters mansion cupola.

The suspended Origami swans (E6) were donated by Member Robert Harbin (1908-1978) who was an expert on the Japanese art of folding paper. These particular "floating swans" were constructed out of metal.

E7, E8, E9, E10

Robert LaPlaine, in association with Jim McKee, designed and created four bare bones magician displays (E7, E8, E9, E10) that recreate famous illusions in magic: The Guillotine, Irma Playing the Piano, The Levitation Illusion, and Senator Crandall's Rope Trick. The loving attention to detail is amazing. The first display was donated in 1968, the other three in 1969 and are testaments to: "If you don't touch it, you won't have to dust it" philosophy.

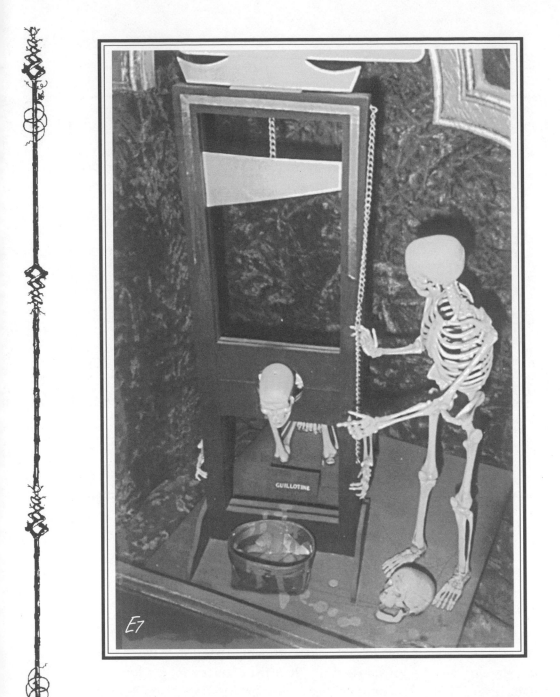

The Guillotine Illusion (E7), is one of the oldest illusions, presented for the first time in recorded history in 1584. In this illusion, a victim's head appears to have been removed from its body.

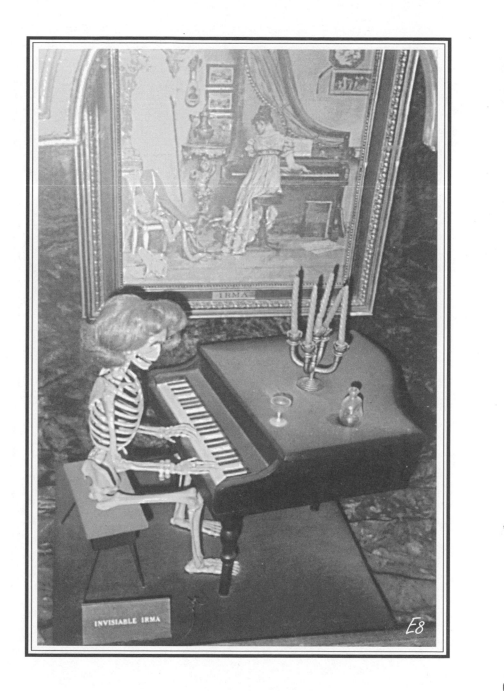

Irma (E8) plays "The Magician Gavotte" while reminiscing about her more visible days in Chicago.

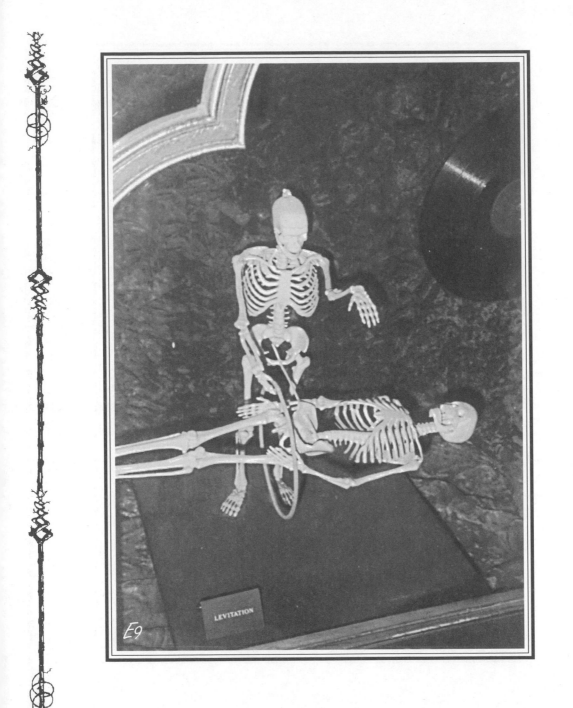

E9

The Levitation Illusion (E9) displays the levitated victim as it floats in air while the magician encircles the form, head to toe, to show there are no visible means of support. The initial Levitation Illusion performance was credited to John Nevil Maskelyne (1839-1917).

The spectacled magician in this display (E10) is "Senator" Clarke Crandall who, according to Member Billy McComb, had perfected his own unique version of the rope trick.

More lantern slides, (E11) used in a missionary temperance lecture, serve as Irma's bar top. These are illuminated from below and display such slogans as "Alcohol... mixed with gasoline," and "Cigarettes and Women... evil effects," the tempting evils of the era.

E12

E13

Sir William Gilbert (E12) and Sir Arthur Sullivan (E13) are portraits on either side of Irma's bar, painted by Member Dr. Tom Heric. Although Gilbert, himself, was an amateur magician and practical joker, Sullivan (creator of "Onward, Christian Soldiers,") on the other hand, would have appreciated the temperance slides embedded in the bar top.

Modern technology has finally advanced to the point where ghosts could actually be captured on film. Although Irma detests having her picture taken, Pam Young was able to surprise her one night as she was performing to bring you this decisive portrait of Irma doing what she likes to do best: playing the piano. We have placed her photograph (E14) outside Irma's Room so as not to annoy her.

Invisible Irma (1857-1932)

Irma was the eldest of seven sisters and one brother who originally hailed from the south side of Chicago. Irma moved with her family to California in 1908 at the same time a fabulous mansion was completed on Franklin Avenue.

Being the eldest in a family of eight children has few advantages in Hollywood, California. It was a hard life with few pleasures. But Irma's escape was music. She spent hours listening to any music she could get her hands on.

None of Irma's family was musically inclined but Irma, nevertheless, used her hard-earned money to subscribe to a mail-order piano course. Irma seemed to live vicariously through her music and was obsessed with learning to play the piano.

The Lanes, music lovers themselves, invited Irma on numerous occasions to perform piano recitals at the Lane mansion. She fell in love with the Victorian oasis. Irma so loved music that when she died she vowed she would return to the Lane mansion where she was allowed to share her love of music amidst such beautiful splendor.

When the piano was moved back to the music chamber, Irma's ghost returned with it. To the amazement and amusement of our guests, Irma visits frequently to take her place at the grand piano. You can observe the piano keys depress as Irma plays almost any tune you request.

The Museum in the Haunted Wine Cellar

Once the basement of the Lane mansion where old furnaces and store rooms could be found, this room was the first main showroom for the Magic Castle. The theatre originally sat an audience of fifty people for performers who demonstrated stage illusions and magic on a small nine foot stage with a ceiling height of seven feet. Two theatre boxes on either side of the stage were reserved for special guests, including a familiar vampire who enjoyed hundreds of performances in semi-seclusion. The theatre boxes are now gone, and instead, on either side of the stage are display cases of magic artifacts and statuettes.

On some busy nights this room is used as an extra showroom for nonscheduled performers to entertain close-up magic and on the first Monday of every month new magicians present their expertise in an audition for membership before the Board of Directors' appointed Membership Committee to become Magician Members.

Original Palace of Mystery Theatre

Bill Larsen

𝕭ill Larsen, Jr. performs in the old Palace of Mystery.

Milt performed his "Gentleman Carpenter" act on the last night they closed the Haunted Wine Cellar as the main theatre. The act started in its usual way but it soon got out of hand. Instead of using a little hatchet, Milt wielded a regulation fire axe and "accidentally" tore out part of the sheet rock ceiling. He performed a "cut and restored" board and the Skilsaw-ed right through the stage floor. As the debris fell, the audience members edged towards the exit. Madness had overcome the performer. Little did the audience know that Milt had planned all along to convert the Haunted Wine Cellar into a museum. It turned out to be an apropos finish to what had been the main showroom of the Magic Castle for many years!

F1-F9

The walls on either side of the old showroom became display cases. The left side exhibits rare and antique magic props seldom used today but they remain memories of a bygone era in magic.

The Magic Linking Rings, Cups and Balls, Rice Bowl and other apparatus (F1-F9) were manufactured by Thayer, Martinka, and Petrie Lewis and were once owned by world famous magicians including Harry Houdini, Harry Blackstone and others.

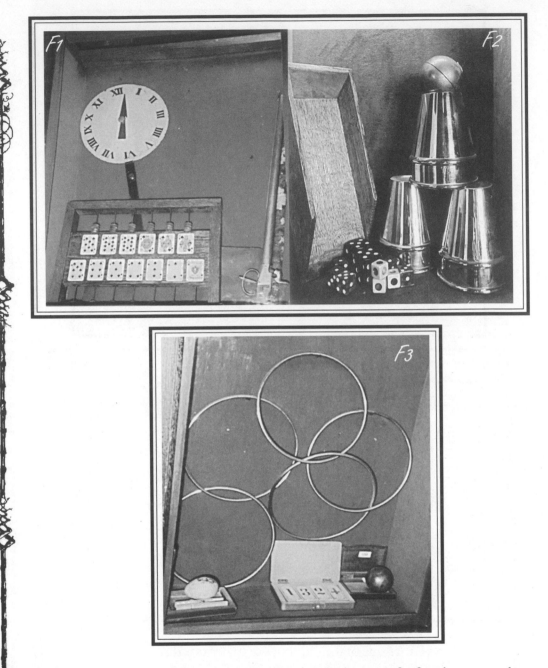

This display (F1) contains a mystery clock, part of a faro layout, and a silk gun.

Cup and Balls, (F2) one of the oldest magical effects, appears in recorded accounts in Rome, Greece, as well as ancient Egypt. A Klingl card ladle rests against the back wall of this display.

Magic Linking Rings (F3), whose origins are vague, were introduced to the Western world by touring Chinese performers. An ordinary-looking 2" metal ball, "The Hot Ball," when held by a spectator, becomes too hot to handle.

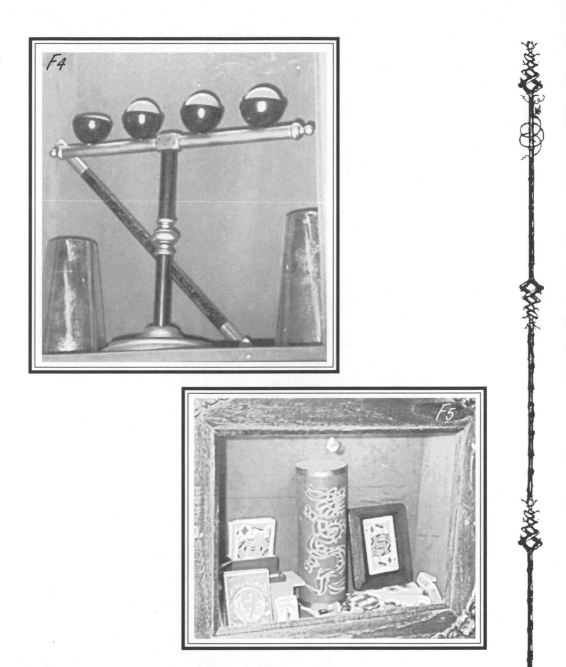

Floyd G. Thayer (1877-1959) was a magic manufacturer who was noted for his high quality handcrafted apparatus such as this small Billiard Ball Stand (F4). Austrian Rudiga Michael Klingl opened a magic shop in Vienna and sold Hofzinser inventions and his Klingl funnels.

A blue dragon "Golden Tube," a glass penetration illusion, and a Thayer card frame with a King of Diamonds are displayed (F5) with Arabic playing cards.

F6

F7

Thayer's Card Dial (F6) magically stops on the spectator's selected card while the antique cast iron magician coin bank merely makes your coins disappear from under his hat.

Lewis Davenport (1883-1961) was a British magician who was equally well-known as an inventor. His imported Thimble Holder is displayed in (F7).

⟜⟩⟨⟜ A confetti hand vase of Conradi-Horster stands stoically amidst various wands including a Coin Wand of Guybert (F8).

⟜⟩⟨⟜ Francis Martinka (1843-1924) was born in Prague. He moved to United States in 1872 and, with his brother, were pro-dealers in NY from 1873-1917 when they sold their manufacturing business. The Bang Gun (F9) was one such manufactured Martinka prop. An antique Hirst ventriloquist's puppet shares the display case.

F10

Robert Stull (1893-1981) was a master mechanic and invented one of magic's most ingenious effects, "The Barrel Illusion" (F10). What looks like a vintage wine barrel is in reality a masterpiece of magical engineering. Robert also invented "The Stull Watch," "The Stull Fishbowl," "The Stull Bullet Catching Effect" and the "Stull Cigarette Gimmick" which were marketed through his Stull Magic Company.

F11-F18

On the right side, the display cases offer a fascinating 1980 collection of hand-molded porcelain statuettes created by Katlyn Miller Breene.

These delicately detailed sculptures feature famous illusions throughout the ages: from the early days of witchcraft and sorcery to modern illusions. (F11) Kellar's Butterfly, (F12) Asrah Levitation, (F13) Dion Fortune, Mistress of Magic; (F14) Katlyn's self-portrait as "The Electric Woman," (F15) Adelaide Herrmann, and another self-portrait (F16), The Occult (F17), and Madame Blavatsky (F19) are among the special displays. Katlyn was an advisor to Copperfield and other grand illusionists.

Katlyn's sculpture (F11) depicts Kellar's latest wonder "The Golden Butterfly" from Harry Kellar's (1906) poster advertising his program of the most daring illusion of the age.

Asrah Levitation (F12) was invented by Servais LeRoy and Katlyn's rendition of the classic illusion uses an Egyptian theme.

━━◇◆◇◆◇◆ Dion Fortune (F13) was born Violet Mary Firth (1891-1946) in England and was a famous writer, having penned "The Mystical Kabbalah," as well as a well-known British occultist.

━━◇◆◇◆◇◆ The self-portrait of Katlyn (F14) as the "Electric Lady" represents Katlyn prior to retiring in 1988 after performing around the world.

~*~ Adelaide Herrmann (1854-1932) was the Queen of Magic (F15). She assisted her husband Alexander Herrmann (1842-1896) until his death when she continued performing solo.

~*~ Another self-portrait of Katlyn (F16) shows her as she performs "The Fire Dance."

~*~ Additional articles of the occult, with Satanic overtones, appear in this display (F17).

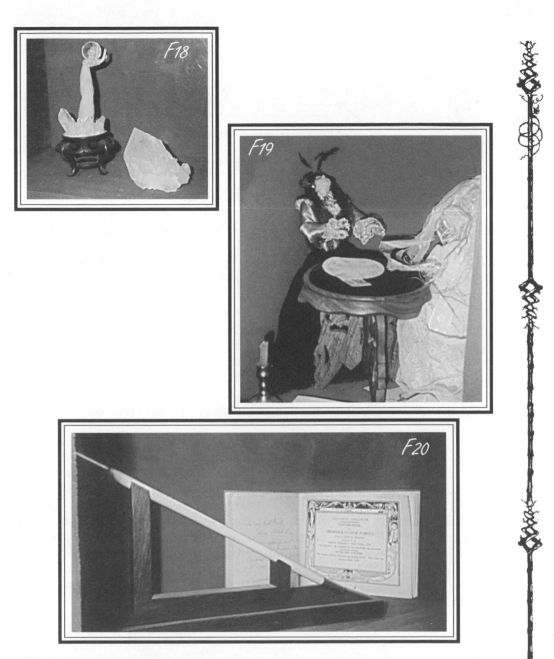

A raw, natural bed of crystals gives birth to a hand holding a refined crystal ball (F18), symbolic of the history of occult crystals.

Madame Blavatasky (F19), from Russian heritage, was born in 1875 in New York and was the cofounder of the Theosophical Society. She was a charlatan in the spiritual community before becoming an occultist.

Frederick Eugene Powell (1856-1938) wrote one book: The Man & His Magic (F20). He was a school teacher turned pro since 1876 and was named Dean of American Magicians in 1922.

William Larsen, Jr. (1928-1993)

Members at the Magic Castle simply called him "Bill." Along with his wife, Irene, Bill was always the guiding force behind the Magic Castle's success.

William Larsen, Jr. was born in Pasadena, California on May 8, 1928. He attended various schools in Pasadena, Arcadia and Los Angeles, before enrolling at Occidental College where he received his Bachelor's Degree.

Since his father was an attorney, Bill, Jr. enrolled in the University of Southern California Law School, but left after his first year, deciding that law was not for him.

Bill found employment as a script typist for the CBS mimeograph department. Shortly thereafter, he transferred to CBS Television Studios where he was employed as a clerk in the cost control department. He then became the head of the entire department and was later transferred into programming, where he worked as a Production Supervisor for the "Climax" television series. Bill became an Associate Producer for the show and continued in this capacity for "Playhouse 90" and variety shows with Danny Kaye and Jonathan Winters. After that, he continued as the Associate Producer for six major television specials on various networks, but found himself at a crossroads with the opening of the Magic Castle. After a few years, as the new club was demanding more and more of this time, he had to make a decision of whether to stay in television or to devote himself full time to magic. His decision was to run the Magic Castle and continue Genii Magazine, and he was never sorry.

92

When Bill's brother, Milt, told him that he had found a marvelous old mansion on Franklin Avenue, the wheels started turning. Many ideas came to mind, but both Bill and Milt remembered their father's dream and decided to try opening a private club for magicians.

While Milt and John Shrum renovated the Magic Castle and created the decor, it was Bill who founded the Academy of Magical Arts, Incorporated, and set to work from the first day to organize the membership, file the applications and to be sure that the daily business of operating the club was being done properly. For some time, Bill practically did this alone, but as the Magic Castle grew, the staff was enlarged and now includes over ninety full time employees.

Bill passed away in 1993, leaving Irene and the Board of Directors to continue the operation of the Academy of Magical Arts. The continuing success of the Academy and the Magic Castle is a monument to his memory.

The Haunted Wine Cellar
Hat 'n Hare Pub

Every old haunted house should have a dark and cobwebbed wine cellar and the Magic Castle is no exception. Milt found plenty of antique wine bottles left by a hired hand who used to live up in the attic and had used a hole in the floor as a trash chute. The discovery of a literal avalanche of wine bottles resulted when paneling was removed in one of the bedrooms below. Utilizing all resources, the wine bottles were used as a wall before further renovation eliminated them altogether.

The Hat n' Hare Pub is actually constructed from the parts of various unique British pubs and saloons. The decor was designed by scenic artists from NBC under John Shrum's direction, who created the feeling of stone walls, cobblestone floors and wooden cabinets. Wood was painted to appear as stone, stone as wood. The illusion was so convincing that one Magic Castle guest thought she had stumbled on the uneven cobblestone floor!

eware, the Hat n'Hare is also a cigar friendly club within the club where members and their guests can enjoy a fine stogie while sipping on a glass of vintage port just as it might have been in the days of the auld British pubs.

The Hat n'Hare Pub (G1) was constructed from various British pubs and saloons, mostly purchased during Milt's raids on British antique shops during the building of his Mayfair Music Hall in Santa Monica in 1973.

The practical bar is used for special parties and is especially busy on Hallo-ween when the underground atmosphere lends itself to the eerie festivi-ties. This area was the primary bar when the museum was the main stage theatre.

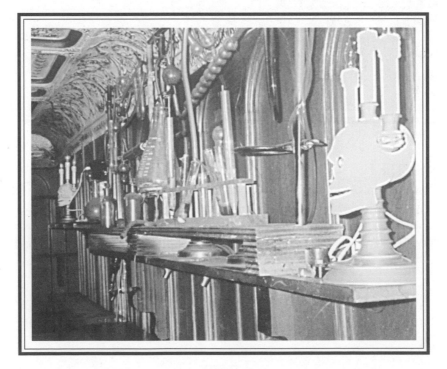

On the hallway wall, prior to entering the Hat n' Hare Pub area, there are several black and white photographs of the Lane mansion and surrounding neighborhood. (G2) is an 1909 street map of Los Angeles, (G3) is Orchid Avenue prior to the Lane Mansion's completion.

(G4) are several photographs of General Harrison Otis' outpost, now the site of the Yamashiro Restaurant, circa 1906. The Lane Mansion is under construction dead center of the largest photograph.

A three-lamp antique gas lamp (G5) is from the MGM Studio auction 1970. The old wrought iron gate (G6), warning those weak of heart not to enter, was an antique store find of Milt's.

G7

The elevator cage (G7) is from a Bunker Hill hotel, named The Frontenac, near the top of Angel's Flight. In the early days of the Magic Castle, the elevator cage was on the mezzanine level. Often various members would stand in the cage, don a mask and remain rigid until an unsuspecting guest would stroll by and then ... Let's just say it was so startling that the insurance company made them stop.

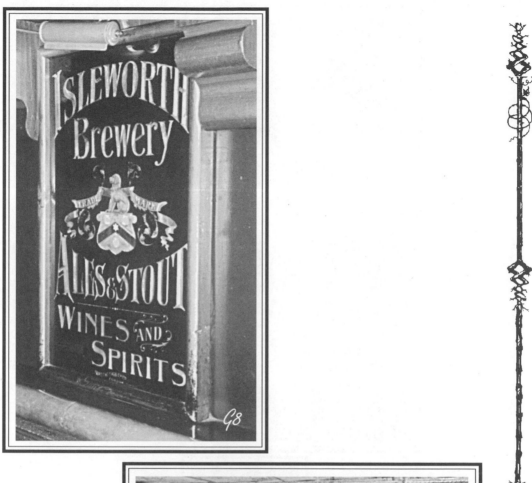

(G8) The Isleworth Brewery advertisement for Ales & Stouts is a typical British pub sign.

The Watney dart board (G9), a regulation British game board, was used frequently in the early days of the Magic Castle when competitions were a monthly event.

Geri Larsen, Bill and Milt Larsen's mother, enjoyed collecting rabbits. At one time she had thousands of rabbits from all over the world. Peterkin, her magic rabbit hand puppet, was used in her act to find the selected card. There are two small collections (G10) of her rabbits in the Hat & Hare Pub area. The original Peterkin puppet resides currently in the Inner Circle display.

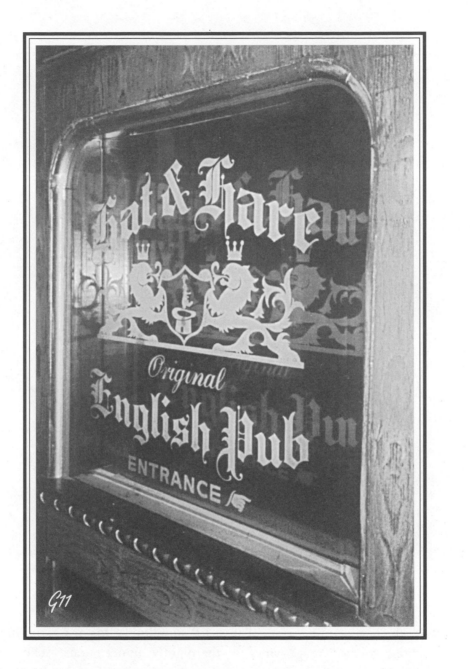

The endless hallway (G11) to the Hat n'Hare was said to be the amazing entrance to Mr. Lane's library. No one who has entered the hallway has been known to return!

G12

The never-ending wine cellar (G12) supplies the Magic Castle with an endless reservoir of vintage wines for the nightly dinner guests. The Magic Castle offers its own label of an excellent Chardonnay and aged Cabernet Sauvignon with an elegant gold embossed emblem of the Magic Castle.

The banjo (G13) in the pub area is handmade by Senator Clarke Crandall (1906-1975). "The Senator" was one of the Magic Castle's most eloquent and curmudgeonly hosts with a mordant wit. His portrait hangs near his banjo (G14). "The Senator" was well-known for his Six Card Repeat. The Senator began as a bar magician in Ray Dauberville's Lounge in Chicago and was friends with Al Capone. Crandall managed Al Sharpe's Magic Shop in Chicago before moving to Hollywood in 1970.

The juggling mouse (G15) was one of John's little creatures hiding within the painted walls of the Haunted Wine Cellar.

G16

John Shrum personalized his basement decor creation by placing his signature card (G16) in one of the apothecary cabinets painted on the back wall.

An evil eye may be watching you from behind the gate! (G17) But another of John Shrum's mice may scare him away.

An old cash register (G18) accents the Hat n' Hare Pub decor.

➤❁❁❁ Cobwebs and wine bottles are realistic illusions (G19) that help create the ambiance of the Hat n' Hare Pub.

➤❁❁❁ A gargoyle lamp (G20) dimly lights the Hat n' Hare Pub prior to entering the improv portion of the pub.

More caricatures (G21) line the dank, cold stone walls in the cobble-stone hallway that leads back up to the Close-Up Gallery. If you feel a chilly breeze through the Haunted Wine Cellar, it may be one of the numerous ghosts that reside here.

One small furnace front (G22) can be found in the Hat & Hare Pub area while the room that leads back upstairs to the Close-Up Gallery utilizes another large furnace front (G23) that enriches the decor. Although both are antique, neither are or were actually used in the Lane mansion.

A skeleton (G24) in the master booth controls the mysteries of the Magic Castle, constantly babbling to himself as he works. It is the creation of Emmy Award winning sound technician James Gordon Williams, a member who is Milt's sidekick on many gimmicks and projects throughout the Castle.

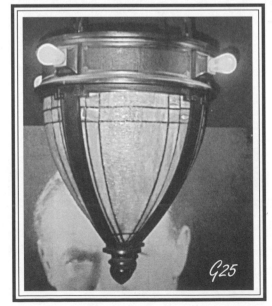

The acorn lamp chandelier (G25) that hovers above the bottom landing of the stairway was purchased from the MGM Studios auction and once graced many a movie set in the 1930's.

Several antique radios (G26) are part of the collection donated by the DeBras in Torrance.

A black and white photo (G27) of Harry Houdini (1874-1926) was the last theatrical picture of Houdini, taken in the Fall of 1926. It hangs in the landing of the stairway leading up to the Close-Up Gallery. The world renown daredevil escapologist was the greatest of his time.

Elvira, Mistress of the Dark, is one of the newest additions to the Haunted Wine Cellar, lending itself to the original concept of Milt's. The pinball machine (G28) is fully operable and awaiting your skilled touch.

Some of the first guests of the Haunted Wine Cellar had to share their libations with the likes of monsters, vampires, ghosts and bats. Elvira seems to be a preferrable option!

Milt Larsen

Milt Larsen's entire life is based on magic. He was born in Pasadena, California and has always called Southern California his home. While still in high school, Milt started writing jokes. His first commercial job came when he was only thirteen years old, writing signs for Gimpy's Hot Dog stand on Wilshire Blvd., for which he was paid entirely in hot dogs. Milt and a partner, Harrison "Red" Baker, started the Comics Information Service while in their teens, publishing nine comedy booklets.

Milt did not attend college, opting to go directly into writing for radio and television. His first major TV credit was "Truth or Consequences," an audience participation show that provided the perfect outlet for a writer with a "talent to deceive." He started with Ralph Edwards Productions when the program, starring Bob Barker, became a daytime series in 1957.

Sitting in his office at Ralph Edwards Productions, Milt looked down on an old rundown mansion on Franklin Avenue and dreamed about an idea that his father, William Larsen, Sr. envisioned... a private club for magicians. One day he met Thomas O. Glover, the owner of the mansion and he suddenly found himself in the nightclub business. His original partner in the Magic Castle was Don Gotschall, who worked at CBS with Milt's brother Bill. Milt and Don took on the challenge of restoring the old house and building a club on faith, love, personal carpentry skills and no money. Milt's writing salary went into the pot every week, while Don finally had to give up his interest in the fledgling enterprise.

For the first ten years of the Magic Castle, most of the carpentry, bars, windows, plumbing, electrical work and gimmicks were done by Milt himself. Others played golf on their days off, but Milt was building a castle. To this day, when time permits, Milt's happiest times are spent in the workshop creating new magical effects for people to enjoy. He can also be seen occasionally performing his two comedy magic acts, "The Gentleman Carpenter," and his club act of routines formerly performed by Bill, Sr. He has been seen (and unseen) in many movies and TV shows doing his favorite "table cloth yanking gag" bit.

In addition to the Magic Castle, Milt Larsen has produced the prestigious "It's Magic!" shows for over 40 years. He created the Mayfair Music Hall in Santa Monica; founded the Society for the Preservation of Variety Arts and established the Variety Arts Center in downtown Los Angeles.

While working on "Truth or Consequences" Milt met the show's costume designer, Arlene Zamiara. She later became the costume designer for Milt's Mayfair Hall and Variety Arts Theatre's productions. After working so well together on many stage and television productions, they decided to wed in 1987. Milt and Arlene continue to work together in making the Castle magical for all who enter. Milt was an elected member of the Community Redevelopment Agency of the City of Los Angeles Project Area Committee for the restoration of Hollywood. He was also an appointed member of the C.R.A.'s South Park Task Force; a former elected member of the Board of Governors of the Academy of Recording Arts and Sciences; a member of both the Screen Actors Guild and American Federation of Television and Radio Artists; as well as the Writers Guild of America.

There is no mystery to Milt's life. It is a Walt Disney world of "nothing is impossible." It is a world of positive belief. Milt Larsen continues to live in a world of magic. Milt lives in a home on the beach in Montecito with his wife Arlene.

At the top of the stairs, turn right and follow the hall to

The Close-Up Gallery

The hallway leading to the entrance of the Close-Up Gallery was originally the exterior veranda of the southeast turret of the Lane Mansion and contains numerous awards from the City of Los Angeles and the State of California.

Once the music chamber of the Lane mansion, this room was one of only four completed rooms when the Magic Castle opened in 1963. Music was restored to the music room in the form of Invisible Irma before its conversion to the Close-Up Gallery.

Close-up magic is one of the most popular forms of conjuring that includes sleight-of-hand, dealing with cards, coins, cups and balls. Small objects appear, disappear, and change at the magician's will. It is one of the purest forms of magic, utilizing polished and practiced methods of manipulation within an intimate viewing range of an audience. Close-up magic will astound, perplex and richly delight and entertain you.

Jay Ose, a brilliant card manipulator, was the charming host and first entertainer in the Close-Up Gallery. He looked like a con man and had the class of a king. Jay was the key element in making the Magic Castle a hit the first five years it was open. The biggest names in show business brought their friends to see this remarkable little man.

Jay Ose

When the Magic Castle first opened in 1963 Invisible Irma's piano was in the round room, which is now the Close-Up Gallery. Resident Magician, Jay Ose, performed his magic in the home's original dining room, now known as the Invisible Irma Room. In 1965 it was decided to switch the two rooms since the Close-Up Gallery afforded more seating space.

One afternoon the Fire Inspector was concerned about the new "theatre" because there was only one entrance, which was also the only exit. He insisted on a second door. Milt asked him to point to a spot where the new door should be. He excused himself, returned with a fire axe and proceeded to create the new door on the spot. A new fire exit was born and Milt became the talk of the Hollywood Fire Department! That's how things usually happened around the Magic Castle!

One of the portraits (H1) on the Close-Up Gallery exterior wall is of William W. Larsen, Jr. performing. Bill learned magic at the age of nine and assisted with the family magic act. He became the editor of Genii Magazine from 1957 until his death in 1993.

John Joseph Platt (1903-1990) learned magic in 1910 from a Christmas gift: the Mysto Magic set. He performed as "Hadji Baba" at the World's Fair in Chicago in 1933 and toured with the USO during World War II. In his later years, he was a house magician at the Magic Castle. His portrait (H2) graces the hallway leading to the Close-Up Gallery.

H3

▸◆◂ "Senator" Crandall, a colorful bar magician from Chicago, was another house magician and host of the Magic Castle for many years. His portrait (H3) is located with numerous caricatures in the annex of the Close-Up Gallery.

▸◆◂ Don Lawton (1922-1988) was inspired by magic at the age of ten after watching a school show featuring a magician. He taught himself magic from library books. Don was a host of the Magic Castle for over fifteen years and a winner of the Life Achievement Fellowship.

H4/H5

➤✦❖✦❮ The rich inlaid wood panels (H4) of the Close-Up Gallery were originally sliding doors in a Hancock Park mansion, next door to the Wilshire Ebell Theatre, the two decade home of Milt's annual "It's Magic!" shows.

➤✦❖✦❮ The portrait of Jay Ose, (1910-1967), (H5) was painted by Member Maury Leaf in 1967. Jay's favorite force was the seven of diamonds.

The back wall between the caricatures displays a 1909 poster (H6) of a "Moorish Phantasy" for Horace Goldin (1874-1939), The Royal Illusionist of the Tiger-God. Hyman Elias Goldstein aka Goldin was born in Poland. He was inspired at the age of twelve watching a gypsy conjuror. Goldin invented the "Film to Life" illusion, "Sawing a Woman In Two" and the "Buzz Saw Illusion" and was noted for his fast-paced style.

The caricatures (H7) that decorate the walls depict many of the award nominated or award winning performers who have enchanted audiences within this room, conjuring miracles literally inches from their unbelieving eyes. These caricatures were created by Ted Salter until 1995 when Ted retired.

For a brief time, Eric Baldassari carried on in Ted's style. You may recognize many of the celebrity performers like Johnny Carson, Tony Curtis, Bill Bixby, Cary Grant, Bob Barker as well as successful professional magicians such as Siegfried & Roy, Lance Burton, David Copperfield, Doug Henning, Channing Pollock and many others.

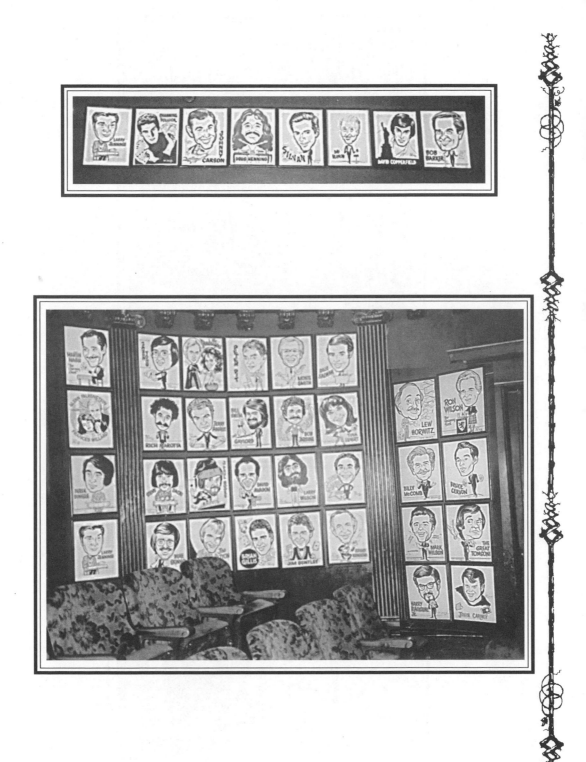

Jay Ose performing magic as a guest star on "The Steve Allen Show."
Steve Allen a Member of the Magic Castle.

Jay Alvin Ose (1910-1967)

Jay Ose is the first performer to have the distinction of being the Resident Magician at the Magic Castle. Born in Echo, Minnesota (a suburb of Minneapolis), Jay, of Scandinavian heritage, became interested in show business at the age of twelve when he joined a traveling medicine show passing through town. A magician, dancer and actor, he continued working until his death in 1967.

During his career, Mr. Ose appeared in many television shows and motion pictures, both performing magic and acting. In 1963, Jay accepted the position of host and Resident Magician for the Magic Castle.

Longtime members remember Jay with fondness, having been impressed with his clever close-up magic and his charming style of performing. Although Jay was slight of build, his sleight-of-hand was brilliant!

Jay took up residence in the mansion for several years. Jay called what is now the Dante Dining Room his home until Milt's renovations became dangerous. He then moved to an apartment that was originally the servant's quarters on the third floor, which was later converted to the William Larsen, Sr. Memorial Library, and is now the Magic Castle business offices.

Jay performed for the nightly guests but is best remembered for his friendly manner of greeting everyone he met. In recollecting Jay's contribution to the Magic Castle, Dai Vernon emphatically stated, "Jay was largely responsible for the success of the Magic Castle." All of the members who knew Jay agree.

Grand Staircase
to The Mezzanine Bar

Dominating the Grand Salon at the north end of the room is the Gothic Staircase that leads upstairs to the four various dining rooms, three theatres, three bars, the business offices, and the Inner Circle.

The photos on the opposite page show how the staircase appeared as Milt began his renovations in 1962 when the entire mansion's interior was white "Zolotone."

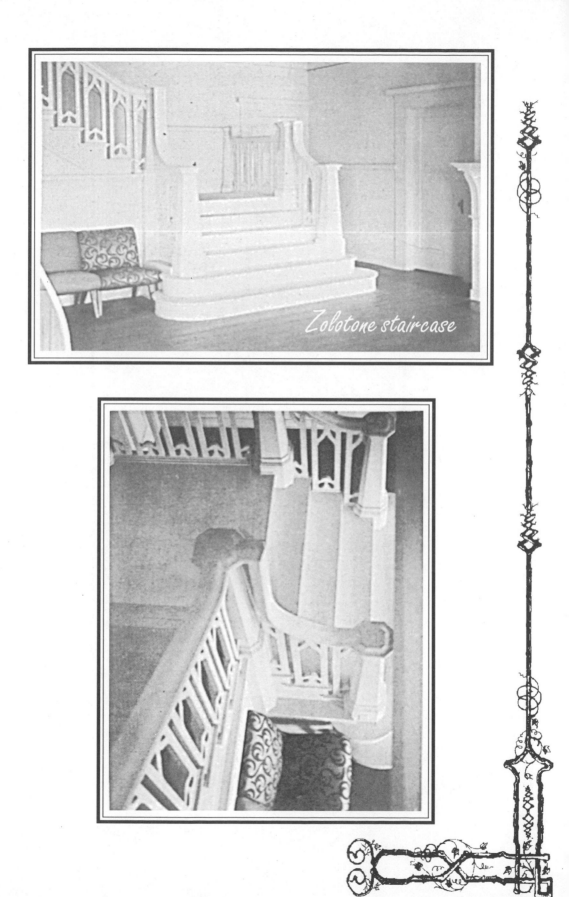

Zolotone staircase

The banister (I1) is original to the Lane mansion however the griffins that perch atop the newel posts originally graced the stairway of the Durand Mansion in Pasadena.

The Durand Mansion griffins (I2) were purchased at an auction by Milt. They were originally on the second floor landing of the huge stairway in the Durand house.

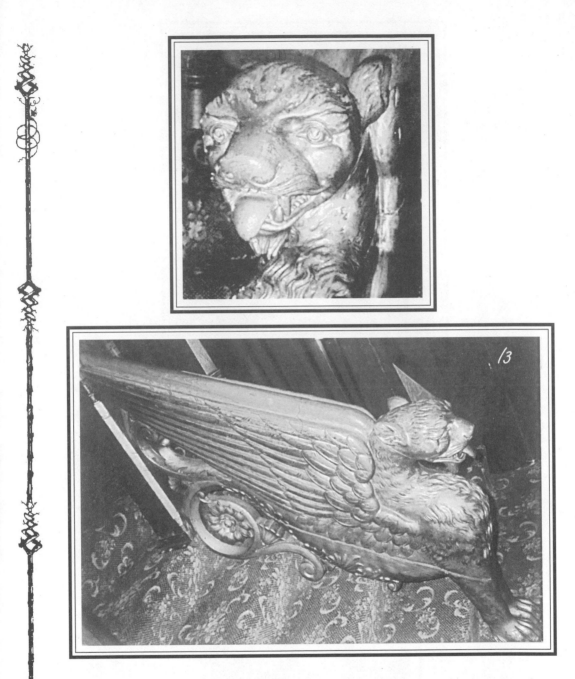

 The large hand-carved lion (13) was from the Borden Mansion (Borden dairy products) in Alhambra, courtesy of Ernie Evans, Scavenger's Paradise. Ernie was an invaluable friend and asset to the Magic Castle with his phenomenal "finds." The lion loves to poke fun at the guests by sticking out his tongue.

14

The eleven-foot-tall grandfather clock (I4) on the center stairway landing is a rare English pipe organ and harpsichord clock circa 1850. The musical part of the clock awaits restoration but you can always count on it giving you the correct time of day. Member Don Kerns, a noted horologist and clock collector, traded the grandfather clock for Milt's 1927 British Alvis roadster. This roadster had also been traded from a long line of antique objects including a Regina Sublima music box and a Mills Violano player (mechanical violin player).

"The Gentleman Carpenter" is a life-sized painting (I5) of Milt Larsen's stage routine which depicts Milt in a white tie, tails and a carpenter's apron while he holds his tools and a martini. Given to Milt as a birthday present from John Shrum, the painting was completed by NBC scenic artist, the late Gerald Mouser in 1968. Gerald later became very well known as a fine and expensive portrait artist commissioned by Robinson's.

The banister lamp (16) is a Victorian lady who lights the passageway upstairs.

The beveled mirror (17) at the top of the staircase belonged to a European castle and was donated by Thalia Phillips, a member and daughter of the first chef at the Magic Castle, Howard Phillips.

The Mickey Finn Show

The Mezzanine Owl Bar

Once the Orchestra Promenade or Orchestra Gallery (a typically Victorian area between floors where a small orchestra or stringed quartet could be easily heard by guests on both floors), this area was the entrance to the William Larsen, Sr. Memorial Library for a year and an impromptu magic table area before being converted to a small intimate bar.

Nicknamed the "Heavy-Handed" Harry's Bar for the bartender of the same name, Harry tried to prove single-handedly that the Magic Castle was nonprofit. The grand old mahogany bar had been shipped "'round the Horn" in 1890 to provide a resting place for the elbows of many a drunken sailor. It found a home in a wrestling arena saloon in Crescent City, California and actually survived a tidal wave in the late 1950's. Milt bought it and, after water damage restoration was completed, the bar was used as a set piece on numerous TV stages including "The Mickey Finn Show" and "The Dean Martin Show" before finding its permanent home as the Mezzanine Bar in 1969.

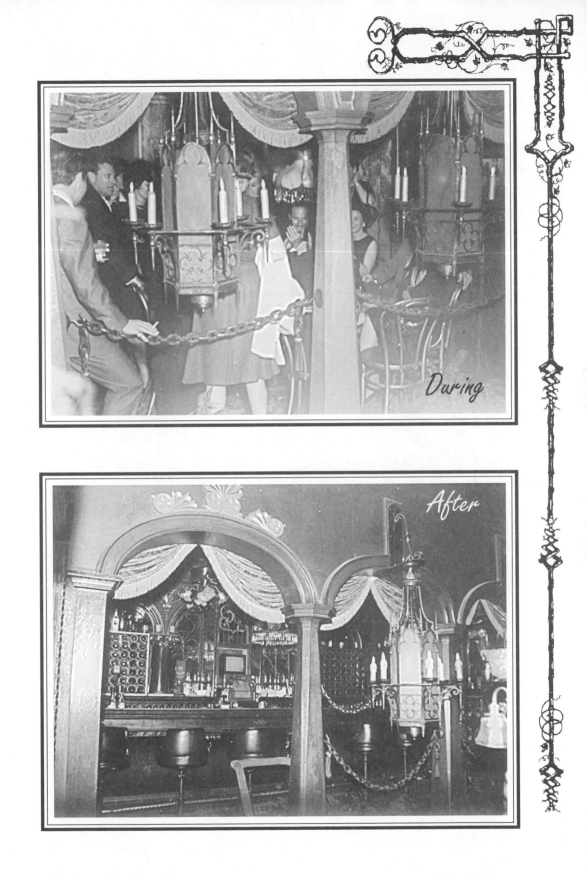

During

After

The far right bar stool of the Mezzanine Owl Bar is still dedicated to and reserved for John Shrum. John designed the Magic Castle and loved to sit in that stool to quaff a few Old Fashions and watch his "standing set" at work. He passed away in 1988 but the warmth of his spirit still blesses those who visit the Mezzanine Bar. A Crepuscular Society plaque declares "May he rest in bitters."

The color photograph (J1) of John Shrum and Milt toasting to their success and friendship at the Magic Castle was taken in 1987 by Al Davis, General Manager. If you look very closely you will see the faint image of Milt's wife, Arlene, reflected in the glass.

 A collage of snapshots (J2) captures John Shrum's very rare magical performance of "Le Petomane," at a "wrap party" for Johnny Carson's "Tonight Show." John was a very shy man who really hated being on the lens side of a camera. This was his one and only performance in his lifetime.

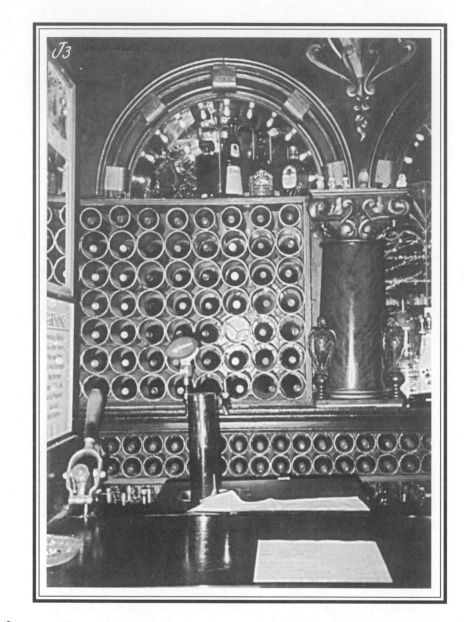

Designed and built by Brunswick, Balke, Collendar (of the bowling lane fame) this bar (J3) represents a "Patented Bar," an order-as-you-go concept where sections of pre-manufactured bar, arches, columns, etc. could be purchased separately, shipped, and fit together at the final destination. It was the standard bar for every high class saloon of the turn-of-the-century.

The Brunswick bar is flanked on both sides with four fireplace mirrors (J4) from the Hotel Frontenac, a fashionable hotel on Bunker Hill near Angel's Flight.

The carved golden oak pillars (J5) are part of the original Lane mansion banister and were discovered beneath plaster walls that separated the mezzanine into an apartment during World War II.

The thistle tin siding (J6) was once a ceiling in a prominent London mansion and part of a shipment from London during one of Milt's Mayfair Music Hall forage hunts.

The wise old Owl (J7) roosting in the center of the arch of the Brunswick bar came from the private study of Harry Kellar (1849-1922) and has a magical ability of its own. He is surrounded by an owl collection donated by various members.

Behind the leaded windows is a scenic backdrop (J8) of Hollywood at night that was used for "The Tonight Show Starring Johnny Carson" when the show first moved to Los Angeles in the early 1970's.

The gold-leafed ceiling floral ornaments (J9) came from the Odd Fellows Lodge, 929 South Hope Street in downtown Los Angeles.

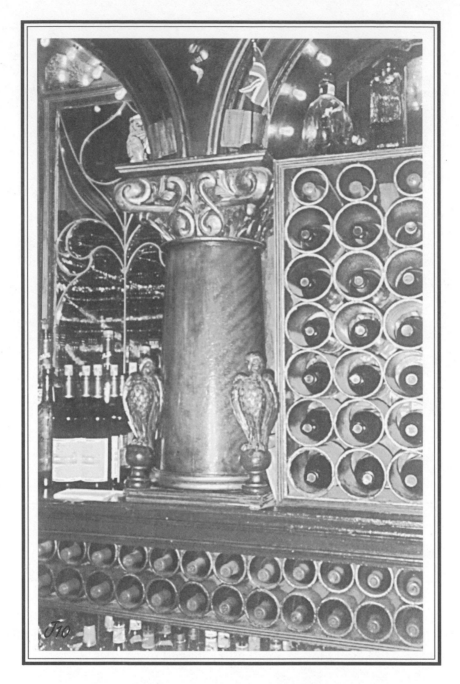

A discerning eye may notice four small hand-carved owls (J10) on either side of the Brunswick pillars. This quartet came from the Women's Athletic Club building on Flower Street, downtown, which was torn down in the early 1980's. They were formerly part of the carved sideboard that is now part of the Dante Room.

The back bar is supported by two pillars and two wine racks (J11). Although it was not the original design, some evil do'er stole the other two pillars the night before the bar was installed. You may also note that the silver emblem and gold lettering, declaring the make of the bar, is not centered. The bar was too long to fit in the Mezzanine space and instead of adjusting the fit from both ends, well... another tribute to Milt's perfection.

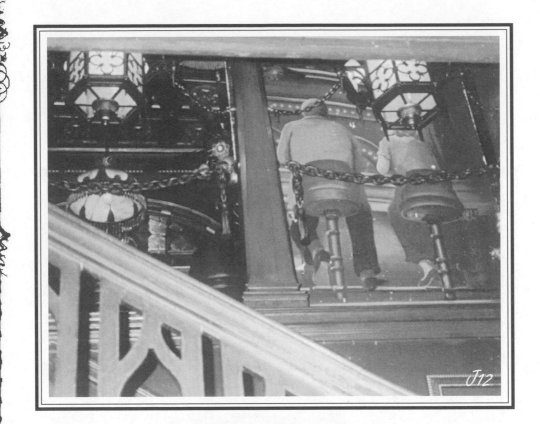

John Shrum designed a pull down shade (J12) of a properly dressed couple to shroud Milt and his worker friends. The lifelike painting masked the worker attired friends violating the coat and tie dress code during the construction of the palace area in 1975.

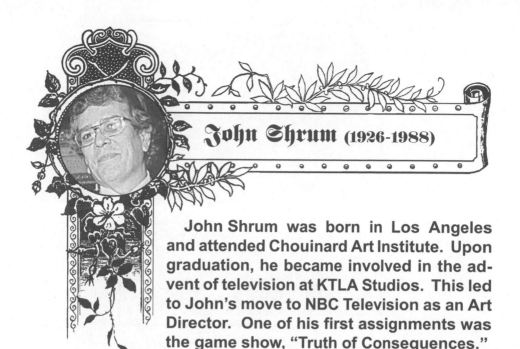

John Shrum (1926-1988)

John Shrum was born in Los Angeles and attended Chouinard Art Institute. Upon graduation, he became involved in the advent of television at KTLA Studios. This led to John's move to NBC Television as an Art Director. One of his first assignments was the game show, "Truth of Consequences."

One day, the writer of the show, Milt Larsen, invited John to the future location of the Magic Castle and from there, everything is history. John's fine sense of design has set the Magic Castle apart from other restaurants and private clubs. The decor denotes class, old world charm, authenticity, and above all: fun!

John became the Senior Art Director for NBC Television. He created the very special and tremendously challenging sets for NBC's most popular perennial program, "The Tonight Show Starring Johnny Carson." He won an Emmy and numerous nominations for his work on this show.

In addition to designing the Magic Castle, John was also Milt's partner in renovating the Mayfair Music Hall which won many architectural awards. He also supervised the restoration of the Variety Arts Center in Los Angeles, in addition to serving as the Art Director for the "It's Magic" shows since 1962.

Main Dining Room

Once the living room, in the parlance of the turn-of-the-century architecture, of the Lane mansion, this room is now the Main Dining Room. The living room originally was very plain. Like everything else in the old mansion when Milt acquired it, the room had been painted with a popular "cover all" paint called "Zolotone," a salt-and-pepper finish that guaranteed to make wonderful old Victorian houses look like brand new post WWII tract homes.

The magnificent dome art glass in the dining room had been stored for years on the roof of Ernie Evans' Scavenger's Paradise building. Originally from a solarium of an old mansion at 3rd and Burlington in Los Angeles, purportedly owned by the Van Stuyvesant family, the dome needed repair and a prominent location to show its true splendor. The entire iron frame was put together with bolts. Each pie-shaped section could be removed and dealt with separately. It took over a week to frame the ceiling and miraculously one late afternoon, the lath and plaster ceiling vanished and the majestic dome appeared. The dome has an appraised value of $35,000 and that appraisal was obtained in 1985. Ernie Evans let Milt "steal" the gorgeous dome for a mere $150.00 — Ernie only wanted to cover his original labor cost. He said he wanted the Castle to have it so Ernie and his friends could sit under it and have dinner!

The parable shape of the dome enables people across the room to hear clearly- so be careful what you discuss during dinner!

 The impressive art glass dome (K1) was originally a roof from a solarium of Van Stuyvesant's mansion. The dome has withstood all the earthquakes since 1963 and even an errant champagne cork David Aguirre, our consummate maitre 'd, shot into the ceiling on a New Years Eve.

To dress up the room, shutters (K2) from the picturesque Norma Talmadge building on Sunset Strip (where LeDome now stands) were cut in half and placed side by side to form vintage paneling. Later, antique mirrors were added to spice up the panels. The master carpenter, Milt, measured the only odd-sized panel and had the mirrors cut to fit. As a result, one fits while the rest are about one inch short; yet another tribute to Milt's perfection.

⊰◈⊱ The art glass (K3) portion of the Victorian Festalboard table was part of the Waters mansion on Adams. The Festalboard™ is a Magic Castle innovation of an array of especially prepared appetizers and salads that can be ordered with dinner or as a separate entrée. Milt coined the word and hired Klaus Risbro, Gerard Roos and Bengt Anderson from L.A.'s famous Scandia Restaurant to create what may have been the very first "salad bar."

David Aguirre, our affable and superefficient maitre'd, (K4) has been with the Magic Castle since 1964. A restoration buff himself, David was featured in the Los Angeles Times (1995) for his restoration of a portion of the Black-Foxe Military Institute in Hancock Park. The Mediterranean Revival-style building once housed the school's founder and headmaster and is now David's home.

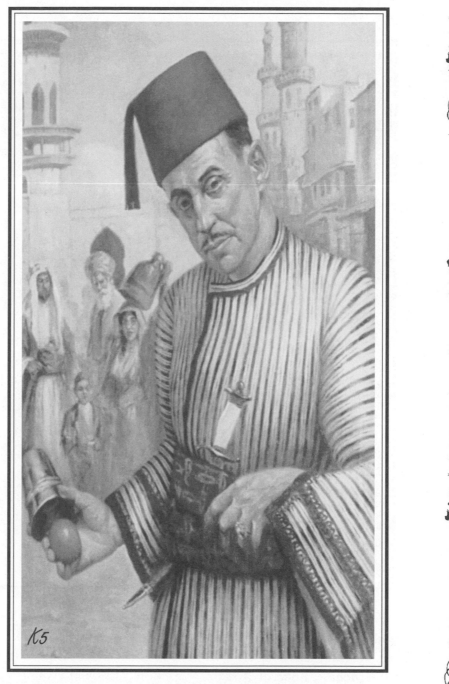

The Salvatore Salla portrait (K5) of "Hadji Baba" is actually magician Johnny Platt (1903-1990) wearing his red fez and authentic costume, including his dragon ring. Member and Platt's good friend, Peter Pit was given a prized, signed Ghandi photograph that had belonged to Johnny but the dragon ring mysteriously disappeared.

K6

By the entrance to the Dante Dining Room is an oil portrait (K6) of South African born magician, Edward Williams, aka Robert Harbin (1908-1978). Member Robert E. Ragatz, M.D. commissioned a young artist, Miguel Paredes to paint the portrait of the magician who is best known for inventing the Zigzag Illusion. Harbin authored two books on the art of Origami and was noted as the greatest inventor of magical effects.

The antique etched windows (K7) that form the room divider between the Main Dining Room and the Cherub Room are from England. Milt made frequent trips to England (for the Mayfair Music Hall) and would bring back a 40' container filled with treasures. The leftovers went to the Magic Castle and this is one such "leftover."

Houdini Seance Room

Once one of the four bedrooms of the Lane mansion, this room was converted into the Houdini Seance Room by John Shrum, Dr. Tom Heric and Milt Larsen on February 27th, 1969. This room is off-limits to most diners due to the private seances in session nightly.

Remodeled in 1997, the centerpiece of this room is a museum-quality, signed Lalique, bronze chandelier that is framed by an ornate golden ceiling. A vintage radio brings back the actual voices of Mrs. Houdini and Edward Saint from that final Houdini Seance in 1936.

A multi-course gourmet dinner is cooked and served at table-side. Seating is limited to ten people to utilize the beautiful Victorian carved chairs, proper silver and china in keeping with the quality one would expect in an elegant home of the Victorian era. Leo Kostka, a renown Magic Castle medium, recreates the final Houdini Seance. Leo enters the minds of the guests and baffles them with feats of mental legerdemain and the appearance of spirit manifestations.

Prior to his death on Halloween in 1926, Houdini made a pact with his wife Bessie, that if it was possible for his spirit to break through the barrier and return to the living, he would contact her. Ever since that day, mediums around the globe have attempted to reach the ghost of the world's greatest escape artist and magician.

Beatrice Houdini, herself, tried for a decade to reach the spirit of her departed husband, with the final official Houdini Seance being conducted on the ten year anniversary of his death, October 31, 1936, on the rooftop of the nearby Knickerbocker Hotel in Hollywood. The seance was only successful in generating publicity.

The Magic Castle, however, has broken through the barrier that eluded Mrs. Houdini and thousands of mediums.

Witnesses from the Houdini Seance have testified that the solid oak table rose several feet into the air... that candles float aimlessly over their heads... that items in locked display cases flew threw the glass, landing inches from their faces... and that they actually saw the spirit of Houdini hovering over them.

The dramatic portrait (L1) of Harry Houdini (1874-1926) by Craig Vilaube dominates the Houdini Seance Room.

The crystal ball (L2), used by Medium Leo Kostka in recreating the Houdini Seance, belonged to Davenport prior to Houdini inheriting it.

Simon Ortega, Harry Houdini's assistant, stored many of Houdini's magic props while Houdini was performing back East. Simon claimed the trunk beneath his framed photos (L3) was given to him by Houdini.

A Substitution Metamorphosis Trunk, 1893, (L4) was purported to have been invented by Houdini and was a mainstay in his early career. The trunk produces an illusion of one performer locked inside the trunk exchanging positions with another outside. When Houdini's assistant, Simon Ortega, turned 100, he proclaimed the metamorphosis trunk to be authentic. His family gave it to the Magic Castle when Simon died. Although the authenticity cannot be confirmed, who can scoff at a Centenarian?

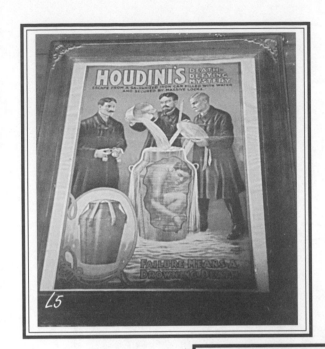

The Houdini poster (L5) illustrates the position that Houdini had to assume in order to perform this illusion.

The Milk Can Escape, 1908, (L6) was another item that was willed to the Magic Castle as an original Houdini prop. The Milk Can Escape was believed to have been invented by Houdini. The milk can is filled with water from the smaller milk cans and the performer is submerged. With the lid securely locked the performer escapes.

_L7/L8_

The straitjacket, typical of those used by asylums at the turn-of-the-century, (L7) was given by Mrs. Houdini to the late Leo Irby who, in turn, donated it to the Magic Castle.

Other interesting memorabilia (L8), located in the display cases around the room, include priceless letters, invitations and photos.

A collection of handcuffs (L9), the likes of which were used by Houdini in performing his escape challenges, are police or military restraints. The Hand-cuff Escape was one of Houdini's first major successes.

A famed invitation to the final Houdini seance at the Knickerbocker Hotel (L10), held a decade after Houdini's death, is obviously very rare.

L11/L12

The ornate Admiral Dewey clock (L11) was presumably owned by the Houdini family.

Member Manny Weltman was the one of the greatest authorities on the life of Houdini. He was credited with the discovery of Houdini's heritage and birth data. Manny was a major collector of Houdini memorabilia. His photograph (L12) holds a place of honor in the Houdini Seance Room.

The antique stove (L13) was found in the attic in 1963 and was one of the original stoves used in the servant's quarters. It has been converted to electric burners and is used for cooking the Houdini Seance table-side dinner.

L13

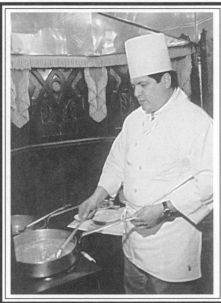

L14

A personal friend of the Larsens, Mrs. Houdini autographed her black and white photo for the Larsen family. This photo dates back to the late 1930's (L14).

The cute little kid in this photo is little Milt Larsen, the co-founder of the Magic Castle, at the age of six. He's doing a fabulous coin trick to amaze a nice elderly lady on the porch stoop. We are sure she was impressed with the trick but she had probably seen her share of magic in her day. The lady was Mrs.Harry Houdini.

Milt's father, William Larsen Sr., served as Mrs. Houdini's lawyer in her later years. She was a charming, diminutive, silver haired woman and an active force in magic. Bessie Houdini devoted her life to keeping the name Houdini alive. Harry Houdini died in 1926. His widow lived until 1943. Every year, on the anniversary of Houdini's death, Mrs. Houdini held a seance to prove whether or not Houdini could come back. The tenth and final Houdini Seance was held, on October 31, 1936, on the rooftop of the Hollywood Knickerbocker Hotel just a few blocks from the Castle on Ivar Avenue. Milt and Bill Larsen's mother and father were part of the "Inner Circle" at the Final Houdini Seance in 1936. Houdini did not come back. or did he?

L15

A black and white snapshot (L15) of little Milt Larsen performing a coin trick for Mrs. Houdini was taken by Geraldine Larsen in 1941 when Milt was only ten years old. Mrs. Houdini passed away three years later in 1944.

L16

L17

HARRY HOUDINI

Presented To
HARRY HOUDINI
on the occasion of the
placement of his star in the
WALK OF FAME
October 31, 1975
HOLLYWOOD CHAMBER OF COMMERCE

Sponsored by
y of Magical Arts

Dr. Edward Saint (?-1942) conducted the final official Houdini Seance, as the medium, in an attempt to reach Houdini. Dr. Saint also handled the public relations and financial affairs of Mrs. Houdini after Houdini's death. His portrait is (L16). Edward Saint lectured about Houdini and was recognized as the person who kept Houdini's name alive throughout the years following his death.

The gilded plaque (L17) commemorates the installation on October 31st, 1975 of Houdini's star on Hollywood Boulevard's "Walk of Fame" for his work as a pioneer in the motion picture industry.

The ornate American reed organ (L18) dates back to the 1900's and supposedly came from Beatrice Houdini's apartment on Vermont Avenue in Hollywood. Arlene Larsen bought the organ from an antique dealer who said it belonged to Mrs. Houdini. Milt cannot substantiate the claim as he was only ten years old when he last saw "Bessie."

The crystal and bronze gargoyle bronze Lalique chandelier (L19) came from a castle in Europe and is valued at over $20,000. The dome has thirteen art glass facets and the chandelier has thirteen lamps. Glenn Evans, son of Ernie Evans and one of Hollywood's top FX technicians, meticulously restored the chandelier, designed and created its Tiffany -style ceiling aperture.

Most escapologists were also stuntmen. Houdini was no different. At Digger's Rest in Melbourne, Australia, Houdini flew the B2 Voisin Freres biplane (L20) in its first sustained flight on the 3rd of March, 1910. He set a new time record of 7 minutes, 37 seconds a mere five days later.

Houdini appeared in a 1919 film entitled, "The Grim Game" (L21) in which the two stunt biplanes collided by accident and were captured on film.

THIS GOTHIC DOOR KNOCKER
WAS FOUND IN THE ASHES OF
HOUDINI MANSION WHICH WAS
PARTIALLY DESTROYED BY FIRE.
THE HOUSE WAS THOUGHT TO BE
HAUNTED AND WAS TORN DOWN
IN 1971. THE PROPERTY ON LAUREL
CANYON BLVD. REMAINS VACANT.

L22

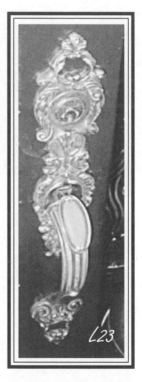

L23

Houdini lived in a guest house in Laurel Canyon. The door knocker (L22) is the only item left when the house burned down in the early 1940's.

The brass door handle (L23) was originally from the Waters mansion's front doors. The handles once graced the entrance doors to the Magic Castle and were moved during the renovation of the Houdini Seance Room in 1997.

Harry Houdini (1874-1926)

A master of publicity, in later life, rumors and legends vary about Houdini's early childhood. However, Houdini was born in Budapest, Hungary on March 24th, 1874 as Erich Weiss, of Hungarian-Jewish parents

Erich Weiss left this world 52 years later with a reputation as the World's Greatest Magician. Whether he truly was the greatest is debatable. The fact remains he was the highest paid performer in Vaudeville and was certainly the best known magician in history.

Building a name on his ability to escape from any lock, jail cell or restraint, Houdini could draw huge crowds with spectacular publicity stunts. In a daredevil style, Houdini escaped from straitjackets while suspended hundreds of feet in the air, was manacled and thrown into rivers, miraculously freed himself from the world's most notorious prisons and performed nightly challenges including the famed "Chinese Water Torture Cell."

Houdini enhanced his reputation by producing a series of silent motion pictures (circa 1918) in which he always played a hero who needed to escape from impossible circumstances to save the day.

In his later life, Houdini became obsessed with the possibility of contacting the spirit world. The results of his research included the expose of fraudulent mediums and even testifying before the United States Congress regarding mediums who were preying on the gullible public.

On October 1926, while on tour, Houdini suffered internal injuries as a result of a blow to his abdomen, but refused to cancel his shows to have surgery. While performing in Detroit, Michigan, Houdini collapsed and was placed in a hospital following the performance. Although the doctor removed his appendix, it was to no avail. Houdini died the following day, and true to his passion for publicity and mystery, it was on Halloween 1926.

Cherub Room

East of the Main Dining Room, once the master bedroom of the Lane mansion, this room became a dining room in 1965. A cherub sideboard buffet was perfect for this room which gave John Shrum the idea to decorate with cherubs.

John Shrum was quite a remarkable magician in his own right. If the Magic Castle needed something special, like a Victorian-style painted ceiling, he would wait for an appropriate time when some performer was scheduled on "The Tonight Show" that needed, say, a backdrop of flying angels. When the backdrop was discarded after the show, it made its way up the hill to the Magic Castle and magically adhered itself to the ceiling!

M1/M2

⚔ The chandelier (M1) suspended from the Cherub ceiling is from a mansion in San Francisco and was an additional find of Ernie Evans.

⚔ The cherub ceiling (M2) was yet another product of the NBC scenic artists and had previously accented the stage of "The Tonight Show."

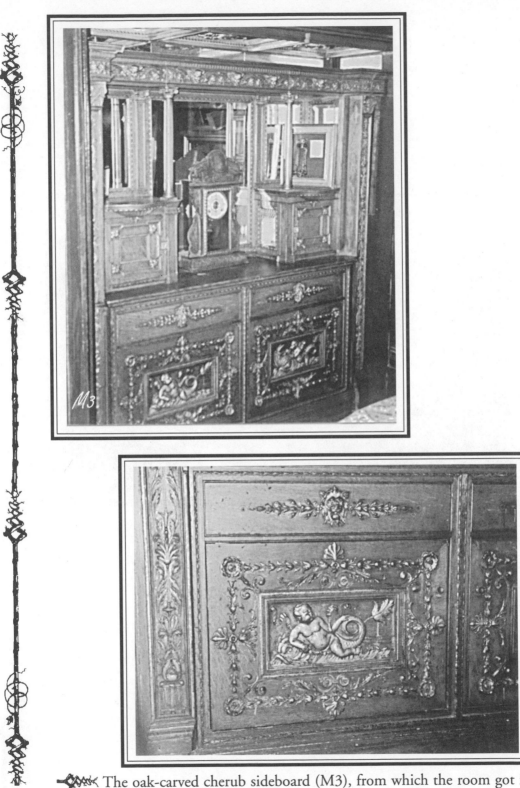

The oak-carved cherub sideboard (M3), from which the room got its name, is from a stately old home in Pasadena.

176

Both the cherub frieze (M4) and the art glass window (M5) were found in an antique store by Milt. The Houdini poster (M6) depicts Houdini performing his handcuff escape routine.

~◆※ Le Grand David (M7) is a spectacular magic company's poster from the Larcom Theatre in Beverly, Massachusetts.

~◆※ Over the years the Castle has accumulated magical themed prints, portraits and paintings such as the golden gilt framed print (M8) of a British manor.

Posters of magicians decorate the Cherub Room walls; the most prominent being a sepia-toned poster (M9) advertising Germain, the Wizard (1878-1959). This rare three-sheet poster dates back approximately to 1912 when Germain was touring the Eastern United States. He was noted as the inventor of the Butterfly Trick. Germain retired in 1911, studied law, and passed the Ohio bar, but unfortunately became blind and spent the latter two-thirds of his life in forced retirement.

Terrace Dining Room

To the south, the Terrace Dining Room was once an open balcony when the Lane mansion was built in 1908. Mr. Lane could sit on the balcony and look down upon the ranch lands of the new community called Hollywood. On clear days, more frequent in the early 1900's, and before the high rises, Mr. Lane could see Catalina. Prior to the balcony being enclosed and expanded it was used briefly when the Magic Castle offered Al Fresco dining. (Milt claimed Al Fresco was a member who preferred eating outdoors.)

N1/N2

The beautiful narrow bays of cut crystal and art glass (N1) were once cabinet doors in a drugstore at 4th Avenue and Washington Blvd., owned by the father of one of our members, Attorney Fred Simmons.

The remaining windows (N2) are impressive acid-etched crystal windows imported from Court Bridge, Scotland, (six miles from Glasgow) where they survived since 1830 as part of the Imperial Restaurant and Pub. Now outlawed as the asbestos of the 19th century, acid etching is no longer practiced.

Robert Burns

If you look closely at the apex of the center window, you may notice a faded portrait (N3) of the great Scottish poet Robert Burns.

N3

~⟨⟨⟨ During the day, solar shades (N4) protect the diners from the glare of the sun. Note that all the shades roll down from one long shaft which is driven electrically by the single motor that once operated the movie screen in the home of the late comedian Herb Shriner.

~⟨⟨⟨ Mahogany columns (N5) were from the old Scottish Rite Cathedral in downtown Los Angeles and enhance the Imperial acid-etched windows.

The exterior bay window at the west end of the Terrace Dining Room was replaced in 1997 with the reception area's art glass window due to very active termites who also enjoyed eating in the Terrace Dining Room.

On the wall opposite the windows is another selection of theatre lantern slides (N6); these from a private collection of film pioneer and one of the founders of Universal Pictures, David Horsley. Mr. Horsley was involved in the purchase of the almost worthless ranch land just past the stagecoach stop on Cahuenga Pass. The lantern slides were illustrations Mr. Horsley used in augmenting a lecture presentation called "Can Anything Good Come Out of Hollywood?" The collection was donated by Member Bill Smith.

One of the lantern slides depicts a signboard announcing the future construction site of Sid Grauman's Chinese Theatre (N7). Real estate offices, including Sphinx Estate Company, offers choice lots in Hollywood and West Los Angeles for $30 down and $350 per lot!

Color fairy tale lantern slides (N8) depict the likes of "Little Red Riding Hood" and "The Three Bears." These very rare, hand-tinted slides came from England circa 1880.

The paneling (N9) that divides the theatre traffic from the dining guests was originally the balcony railing of the Waters mansion and the actual doors into the main dining room. The doors were best utilized on their side with the ornate railing on top.

Ten dome ceiling lamps (N10) were purchased from the MGM Studios auction and were primarily used in railroad station scenes during the 1940's.

The Terrace Dining Room has seen many changes and renovations through out the years. The display cases have changed, the flow of theatre traffic has been diverted from the diners, but the view has remained the same and continues to be the most popular eating area of the Magic Castle.

Irene Larsen

Irene Larsen was born in Stuhlingen near Munich, Germany and was raised in Austria and West Germany. She learned stage magic in 1956 as an assistant to John Daniel and moved to United States in early 1957. Irene subsequently married John Daniel.

It was Irene's beauty and onstage presence that persuaded Orson Wells to ask her to perform the Disembodied Princess with him on the "Dean Martin Show."

Bill Larsen met Irene after their first marriages had dissolved and they were married on November 10, 1963. They have four children: Wendy, by Bill's first marriage; Dante, by Irene's first marriage; Heidi and Erika, from Bill and Irene's marriage and two grandchildren; Jessica and Libby.

From the first day the Magic Castle opened its doors, Bill and Irene were there. Irene learned close-up magic from Jay Ose and has always been an ardent supporter of the Magic Castle.

The initial success with 151 members on its opening day, to the present status of over 5,000 members, can be attributed to the hard work of Bill and Irene Larsen.

In addition to their executive and social positions at the Magic Castle, Bill and Irene traveled all over the world, working as Ambassadors of Goodwill from the Academy of Magical Arts and Genii Magazine. Irene is also an avid animal lover and is very active in several organizations preventing cruelty against animals. Each year, she and television celebrity Bob Barker host a charity benefit for these groups at the Magic Castle.

An animal activist, Irene is adamant that magicians treat their animals humanely. The first placemats used at the Magic Castle depicted a magician lifting a rabbit from a hat by its ears. Irene insisted on changing the design to show a more humane presentation.

Irene has served on the Board of Directors and continues to travel worldwide to represent the Magic Castle and remains an ambassador to magic. She is Honorary President for Life.

Dante Dining Room

Originally one of the four bedrooms of the Lane mansion, this room was home to Jay Ose for several years prior to opening as the Dante memorial dining room on Halloween 1965. It was designed by John Shrum and executed by NBC's Oma Lee and Borden Newman.

This room is dedicated to the memory of Dante who was an ultimate magician performing in a magic revue, in contrast to Blackstone who performed a whirlwind vaudeville act. Dante was an internationally acclaimed magician and personal friend of the Larsens.

The Dante Dining Room is used throughout the week as one of our most popular dining rooms as well as the main buffet area for Sunday brunch.

 The walls are comprised of panels (O1) from a Hancock Park mansion next door to the Wilshire Ebell Theatre. The house was torn down in 1965 to provide a parking lot for the theatre and happened to be rescued by Ernie Evans and Milt, along with the wrought iron handrails leading to the Inner Circle and a few chandeliers.

 The panels are decorated with playbills (O2) from the numerous Dante full evening program "Sim Sala Bim" which toured the nation from 1936 through 1938 as the last tour in England, the "Farewell Visit."

 The arched mirror panels (O3) that line the walls and the ornate chandelier are both from a mansion in the Fremont Park district.

➳ A large 1931 hand-colored photograph (O4) advertises "The Mysterious Dante" and was used in the theatres' lobbies in England during Dante's tours.

The Dante's Inferno ceiling (O5) is similar to the one in the Grand Salon, painted by NBC artist, Jim Dodson.

The wall sconces (O6) are one-of-a-kind fixtures manufactured by Milt in his workshop in Santa Barbara from interesting mahogany and beveled glass he had collected. Typically Milt couldn't find the fixture that would do what he wanted so he simply created his own.

The built-in sideboard (O7) was originally from the Los Angeles Women's Athletic Club on Hope Street, constructed in 1924 and torn down in 1980.

Alvin Jansen, Dante's son, was the artist for his father's poster (O8).

Dante (1883-1955)

Born Harry Alvin Jansen in Copenhagen, Denmark, Dante was one of the greatest magicians of the 20th century. Brought to United States at the age of six, Harry was inspired seeing a performance of Leon Herrmann. Harry debuted as a magician in 1900 and began his first professional World Tour in 1911.

He toured the various theatre circuits from the time he was twenty. Jansen built his own illusions and props at a magic company he founded in Chicago and began working for the renowned illusionist Howard Thurston in 1923, who gave him the stage name of Dante and sent him touring around the world.

Dante toured internationally for over a decade, before he began his own show, "Sim Sala Bim" in London. Using new, innovative illusions including a "Dancing Waters"-style finale, Dante was a true sensation in his day. After one hundred and fifty weeks performing in Great Britain, Dante decided to move his show to the continent where, after only two months, he and his company had to flee the country within hours of Hitler's invasion.

Dante moved to California in 1940, where he continued to perform both on stage and occasionally in the movies; his most famous film appearance was in the Laurel and Hardy comedy, "A Haunting We Will Go" (1942). Dante passed away at his ranch in the San Fernando Valley in 1955. During his lifetime, Dante performed on all five continents and established more theatrical records than any other performing artist at that time.

Palace Hallway Art Gallery

The Thomas O. Glover, Sr. Annex was formerly the center of a parking garage added in 1963 to provide a solid road to the Yamashiro Restaurant and an underground parking facility for the Magic Castle.

Once again, John Shrum displayed his architectural genius in camouflaging the old with the new annex. The photos by the kitchen doors are old black and white photographs of the Lane mansion and neighboring areas.

Photographs, portraits, and posters fill the hallway walls of current and well-known magicians, illusionists, manipulators including Harry Blackstone, Franz Harary, David Copperfield, Doug Henning, Dom DeLouise, Mark Wilson and Chuck Jones, just to name a few. There are also fascinating 3D and Holographic displays. The art gallery is constantly changing.

P1

One photo (P1) exhibits a small gazebo where General Harrison Otis, founder of the Los Angeles Times, used to ride his horse to meditate daily. The General (presumably a General from the Spanish American War) called it his outpost. The route that General Otis took through the canyon to the top of the hill is now called Outpost Drive.

The second black and white photo (P2) of the Lane mansion was taken in 1938. Notice the large lawn in front and the turret that was the western edge of the balcony. Milt can only guess whether the gentleman descending the stairs is Rollin B. Lane. If you look back toward the Terrace Dining Room you will notice the enclosed turret (P3)... which means that right now you are standing on air. The western-most turret of the Lane mansion at the entrance to the kitchen, was once an exterior wall.

P3   Turret

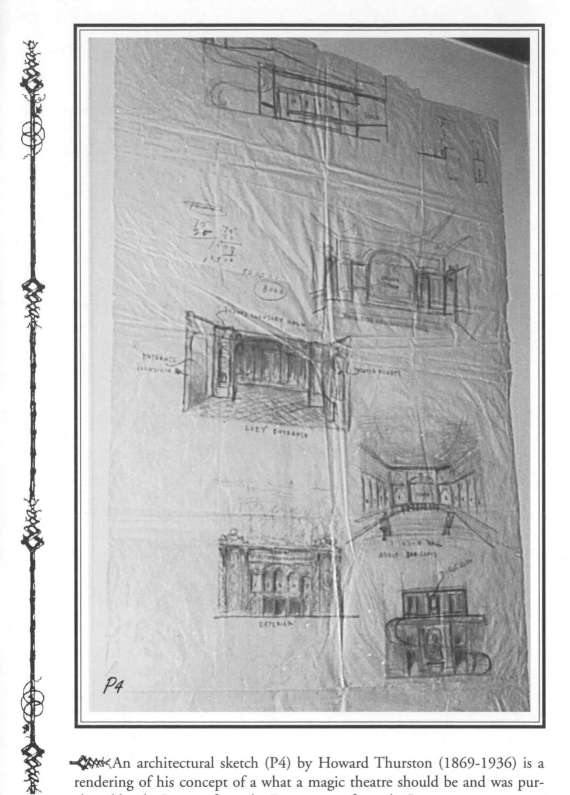

An architectural sketch (P4) by Howard Thurston (1869-1936) is a rendering of his concept of a what a magic theatre should be and was purchased by the Larsens from the Dante estate from the Jansens.

The Amazing Kuda Bux (1905-1981) was a Indian from Kashmir "with X-ray Eyes" who introduced fire-walking into the world of magic. The portrait (P5) was painted by Margaret Hugh.

Salvatore Salla provided another oil portrait of Johnny Platt (P6) as "Hadji Baba."

Salvatore Salla's self-portrait (P7) was painted in 1962. Salvatore was a professional magician as well as one of the foremost painters of magic subjects and themes. Many of the wonderful portraits here at the Magic Castle were painted and donated by Salvatore Salla.

The Max Malini (1873-1942) portrait (P8) was loaned to the Magic Castle by his son, Ozzi Malini. Malini was the King of Entertainers, an entertainer of Kings. He was often asked to perform for royalty when he was free. He was never free — he was very, very expensive!

Milt Larsen, (P9) dressed in tails, dances with his top hat and bang gun. The photograph was taken for a German magazine featuring "interesting people in Hollywood."

"SALLA'S MAGICAL MASTERPIECE OF THE GREAT MASTERS"

P10

"The Magical Masterpiece of the Great Masters," (P10) 1979, is Jack Gwynne's Levitation Act with members of the Royal Family of Magic including his wife, Anne, daughter Peggy, son, Buddy and his wife, Helen and three grandchildren while he performs for the great masters of the past: "Okito" Bamberg, Percy Abbott, Harry Blackstone, Sr., William Larsen, Sr., Harry "Dante" Jansen, Howard Thurston, Harry Kellar, Alexander Herrmann, David "Fu Manchu" Bamberg, Dr. Harlan Tarbell, Harry Houdini, and Sorcar of India.

An Art Nouveau Bronze (P11) lady lamp greets you at the bottom of the stairs holding two lavender lanterns.

The Australian illusionist, Levante's poster (P12) dates back to the early 1930's. Levante (1892-1978) claimed he was the modern master of all magic. He was the inventor of the Impaling Illusion.

At the bottom of the stairs that lead into the Palace Bar and Theatre area, you will find another restroom (P13) for the ladies. This room is decorated with flyers of women magicians, period advertisements from turn-of-the-century catalogues.

P14

At the far end of the hall, closest to the Palace of Mystery, is a large color photograph (P14) of Milt and Bill's mother, Geraldine. The photograph dates back to the late 1930's when Mrs. Larsen wore an old-fashioned hoop skirt in the "Larsen Family of Magicians Show" that featured the entire family of Larsens. One of her special bits was the finding of selected cards by a personable little rabbit named Peterkin. Geri was the very first woman ever to perform on television prior to World War II at the Golden Gate Exposition in San Francisco.

Geraldine Larsen

Not only has Geri devoted time, energy and finances to the Magic Castle, she also entertained as "The Magic Lady" on KTLA-TV in the 1940's and had her own syndicated show in the fifties. She also created the Magic Castle founders, William Jr. and Milt.

Geri was born in Traverse City, Michigan on June 1, 1906. She grew up in Michigan, Ohio and Indiana and graduated from high school in Lansing, Michigan in 1923. Her family moved to California where Geri attended Occidental College and subsequently met William Larsen, Sr.

When William Larsen, Sr. founded Genii Magazine in 1936, it was Geri who managed the finances and made sure the magazine got out every month, while Bill did most of the writing. She continued as coeditor of the magazine after Bill, Sr. passed away in 1953 and slowly shifted the duties to William Jr. who eventually became publisher and editor.

Geri kept very active and married radio and TV personality Art Baker, who, although not a magician, featured many magicians on his TV program, "You Asked For It."

Geri has written several books with a magic theme, performed as an actress and has received honorary memberships in scores of organizations throughout the world. She was one of the founders of a club for female magicians, "The Magigals" and was their President in 1939 and again in 1960.

After Art Baker's death in 1966, Geri met retired candy manufacturer Rubin Jaffe. They were married in 1970 and subsequently traveled around the world. Rubin Jaffe passed away in December 1976. Geri always comments on how lucky she is to have had not one, not two, but three wonderful and full lives.

Geri is still going strong, though in her nineties, and lives in Casa Dorinda, a beautiful retirement condominium in Montecito, California. She has every reason to be proud of her contributions to the most unique private club in the world.

Palace of Mystery

As you pass from the long hallway west of the Terrace Dining Room and down the five stairs to the Palace of Mystery Theatre, you are actually stepping out of the original Lane mansion into The Thomas O. Glover, Sr. Theatre Annex that connected the original Lane mansion to the three story parking structure.

The Palace of Mystery is the largest theatre in the Magic Castle, seating over one hundred and twenty-five guests. Originally the second level of the parking garage, the area was converted into a club when the fire department refused to allow more than fifty people into the Magic Castle without the installation of sprinklers.

The Palace of Mystery theatre stage has featured some of the finest names in modern magic from around the world. From levitating beautiful women to mind reading, from dividing assistants in half to hilarious comedy antics, the Palace of Mystery is one of the most spellbinding venues in the world. Three different masters of magic are featured each evening performing feats of magic that leave the audiences amused, amazed and highly entertained.

➤ In the waiting area there are several handcrafted cases donated by Member Mike Elkan as well as a convenient telephone booth (Q1) we suggest you use to check on the babysitter.

➤ The tin walls and ceiling in the waiting area for the Palace of Mystery Theatre (Q2) are from one of the first fire stations in downtown Los Angeles.

Magician posters (Q3) decorate the Palace Lounge walls, including four posters featuring Chung Ling Soo, circa 1900's. These posters are extremely valuable as they were printed in limited editions of only 100 or 200. Chung Ling Soo (1861-1918), a.k.a. William Ellsworth Robinson, prided himself on his posters. Competitions of aspiring art students were held and the artists were invited to design a poster. The winning entry would be used for his show. The Magic Castle is the proud owner of five of Chung Ling Soo's posters (the fifth is downstairs in the Grand Salon).

Chung Ling Soo used his oriental theme throughout his magical presentation. He was a highly creative inventor who was remembered for the artistry of his performances.

Chung Ling Soo was mortally wounded performing the Bullet Catch on-stage at the Wood Green Empire Theatre in London in 1918. Billy McComb portrayed Chung Ling Soo for a BBC special. It was during the filming of this project that Billy learned of the possibility that Soo's death might not have been accidental but premeditated murder committed by Soo's Japanese assistant, Frank Kametaro.

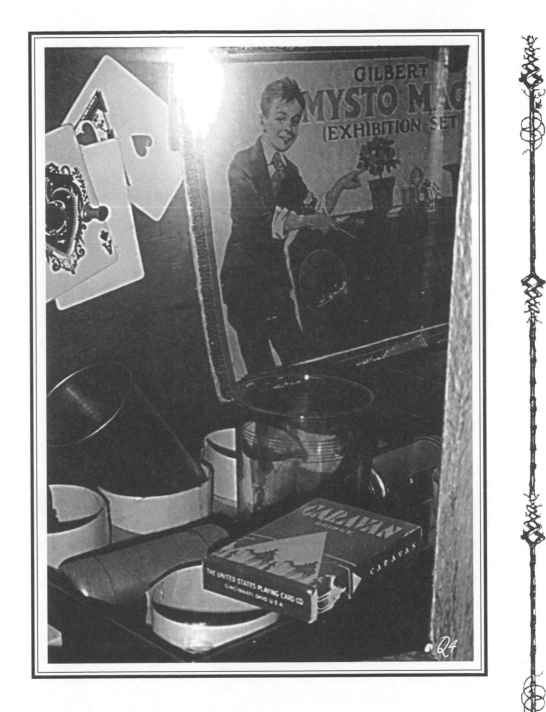

Above and below the Kissing hologram are more antique magic props (Q4). In the 1930's and 1940's, children grew up wanting either an erector set, a chemistry set or a magic set. "Mysto Magic" is one of these sets, manufactured by A.C. Gilbert Company (who also manufactured the erector and chemistry sets).

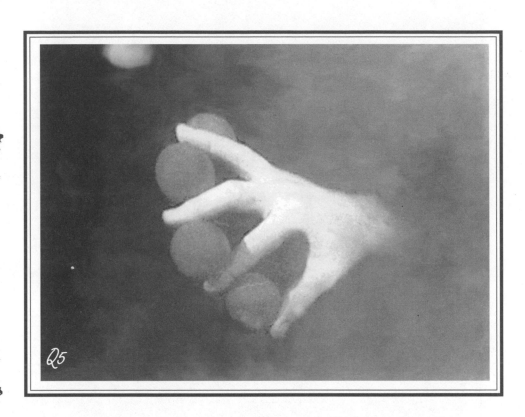

The Hand and Balls (Q5) hologram on the wall came from London, England. John Salisse, a member and VP of Marks & Spenser, (a large store in London) had purchased a one-of-a-kind hologram from a store in Covent Gardens. Milt admired John's and wanted one. He asked for another but John had to agree to the production of the second one which he readily did, making this hologram a "Two-of-a-kind." This is the only hologram ever made with two official first editions.

Venice Pier

Q6

~~~ Once in the interior of the theatre, you may notice the original four concrete pillars from the parking structure. Two of these pillars create the proscenium arch for the stage and are capped with decorative Ionic capitals (Q6) that came from the original pier in Venice, California. The faces are modeled after a beauty queen and a local businessman.

The four parking structure pillars were, obviously, not removable. John Shrum had to work his own magic in incorporating them into the theatre decor to make them literally disappear.

Ernie Evans called Milt one day when the Palace of Mystery was under construction. A large apartment in Long Beach was scheduled to be imploded but there were 300 mahogany doors (Q7) that had been closet doors, Murphy bed doors, and bathroom doors. Such a waste! Milt called John Shrum, who, without a beat, delightedly announced that Milt had just found the paneling for the Palace of Mystery theatre. If you look closely, you may notice little spaces where door handles used to be. There's room numbers, a doorbell, and even one door around that still says MEN on it. They are also reversible. If the front of the paneling wears out, they can be turned around and their backs can be used!

The massive chandelier was once a two-tiered lighting fixture (Q8) from an old Spanish inspired building at Washington and Hope Streets, The Los Angeles Real Estate Association. The Palace could only handle one of the tiers so the Parlour of Prestidigitation has the smaller bottom tier of the chandelier.

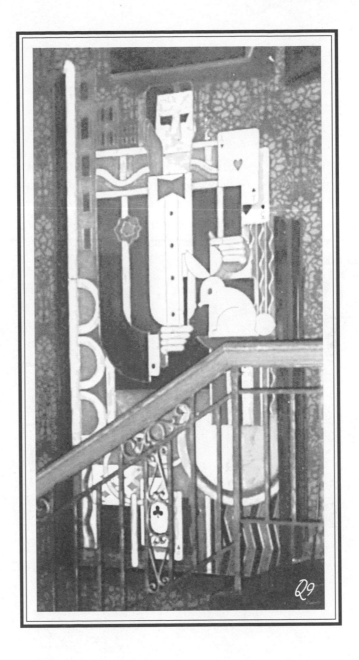

On either side of the stage are two grandiose torchiere lamps (Q9) from MGM Studio. They are most obvious in the MGM film: "The Grand Waltz" and the art glass stage decorations were used for the magic special, "Magician's Favorite Magicians," produced by Milt Larsen and Armand Grant which aired on CBS in 1995.

Palace Bar

The Palace Bar is a sumptuous meeting/lounge area that provides another impromptu close-up table area. The beautiful bar was put together using many pubs and saloons in England. These items were not purchased directly from the pubs and therefore origins cannot be authenticated.

The hand carved bar (R1) dates back to 1830 and was originally part of a pub in King's Cross, a section of London. Milt was only able to purchase the front and the gantry arches but the bar top was missing.

Vintage bird's eye maple from one of the first administration building at Hollywood High School creates the top of the bar (R2). The bird's eye maple dates back to 1901 and was removed when the building was razed in the early 1970's.

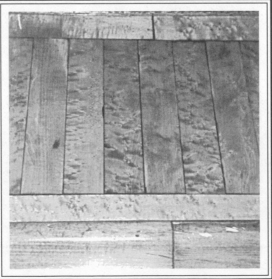

Stamped tin panels (R3) from a lodge hall in San Pedro create the Palace Bar walls while the tin ceiling comes from one of the first fire house stations in downtown Los Angeles. Tin was a typical ceiling and wall dressing in stately Victorian homes.

Perched center in the Palace Bar is a small, dainty Victorian lady bronze lamp (R4) that appears to be flying.

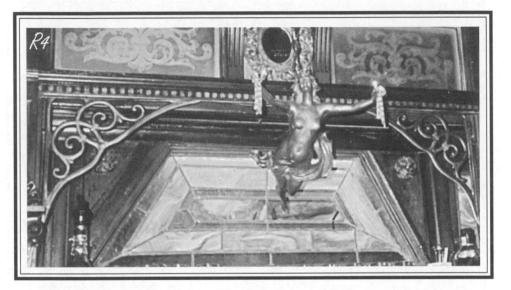

The carved redwood woodwork (R5) above the tin siding was salvaged from a school in South East Los Angeles.

The stained glass (R6) behind the bar is from a church in Whittier that was demolished in the mid 1970's.

The Bullocks Department Store in Southern California used lighting fixtures (R7) in their displays. They now hang as the main lighting in the Palace Bar area.

R8

━✦━ The oil painting: "Magicana" (R8) by the improv table was painted in 1962 by Salvatore Salla and contains a self-portrait of himself in the photograph on the left.

The portrait (R9) of William Larsen, Jr. (1928-1993) was painted by Loyal Lucas in the mid-60's from a photograph that appeared in his Genii Magazine.

Waiting Area of the Parlour of Prestidigitation

The large art glass window (S1) came from the same church in Whittier as did the paneling inside the Parlour of Prestidigitation.

The art glass window (S2) originally came from an old manor in England but Arlene Larsen found it in storage in Santa Barbara. Although Milt had planned on the window being installed in his second story addition to their house in Santa Barbara, the addition has not come to fruition. Milt and Arlene thought the guests of the Magic Castle would enjoy the window more than the mice in their garage. The window dates back to the early 1800's.

The large golden statue (S3) was built in 1938 as a set piece for the Earl Carroll Theatre/Restaurant, which is now the Sunset Blvd. Theatre, formerly the Aquarius, Kaleidoscope, Chevy Chase Theatre, Hullabaloo Theatre and the Moulin Rouge on Sunset Boulevard.

You may recognize the headboard (S4) of Jack Nicholson's bed from the film, "Witches of Eastwick."

A corner of the Magic Castle is dedicated to Dai Vernon, "The Professor" and includes a Viennese street sign (S5) that was given to Dai from a magic club in Germany. It is doubtful that the sign was ever used on the street.

The black and white photo (S6) of Dai as a young man was taken by Hal Phyfe in the 1930's as contrasted with the color photo (S7) taken years later by Young & Robin.

A large oil painting (S8) by Margaret Hugh is also of Vernon with "Cups and Balls."

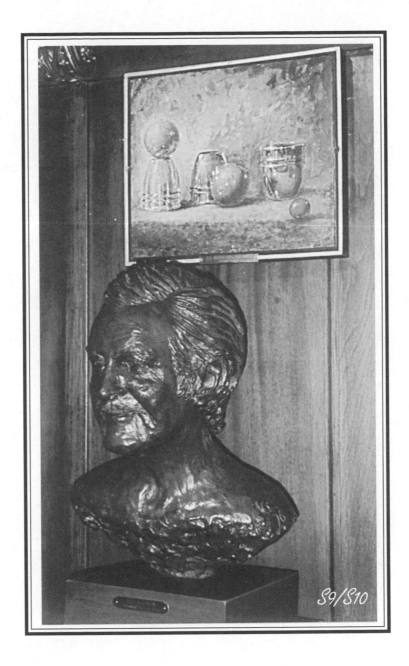

S9/S10

—〇〇〇< A life-sized bust (S9) of Dai Vernon greets you at the entrance to the Parlour of Prestidigitation. The bust was crafted by Yvonne Cross in 1976.

—〇〇〇< The portrait (S10) of Emeritus Board of Directors, Dai Vernon, is entitled "Cups and Balls," and depicts the magic props that Dai made popular.

Dai dedicated a color photo (S11) of his magical props to the Magic
Castle, his "real" home.

Dai Vernon (1894-1992)

On his 90th birthday in 1984, Dai Vernon stated that he had spent 84 of those years doing magic... and that he had wasted the first six years of his life. Nicknamed "The Professor" by close friends, Dai Vernon is recognizable worldwide as the Dean of American Magic. He has been a friend of the greatest names in magic for nearly a century and magicians around the world still respect his skill.

Originally from Ottawa, Canada, Dai's was born David Fredrich Wingfield Verner. He learned magic at the age of eight from his father, an amateur magician. Dai began his professional career in 1913 when he moved to New York and specialized in close-up magic. He made a living as a magician for the next seven decades and authored over a dozen books in magic. He was adept as an artist of silhouettes and found it a profitable profession.

In 1963 Dai came to Hollywood, California to visit his friend, Jay Ose, the Resident Magician for a new club called the Magic Castle. Dai never left other than annual lecture tours and special personal appearances. He is with us, even today, in spirit.

Dai Vernon's expertise and reputation have been recognized by magicians and the public around the world. Dai is considered the mentor of magicians like John Carney, Bruce Cervon and Larry Jennings. The Magic Castle was proud to be considered his "real" home.

Parlour of Prestidigitation

Just beyond the Palace of Mystery is the Parlour of Prestidigitation which opened in 1976. This theatre comprises the second theatre in the Thomas O. Glover, Sr. Theatre Annex which was added from existing space in the parking structure.

The Parlour of Prestidigitation is an intimate stage used primarily by acts that feature and combine small stage effects with close-up magic. Many popular comedy magicians and acts that use audience participation prefer this room, since the audience is only several feet from the stage.

The Parlour of Prestidigitation has a similar decor to that of the Palace of Mystery. A handsome carved proscenium from the turn-of-the-century Odd Fellows Lodge comprises the stage arch along with the rich mahogany door paneling from Long Beach.

The theatre is designed backwards. The audience enters at stage level and sits higher than the performer. John Shrum designed the theatre in this fashion as the ceiling was highest where the artist performs, making the Parlour of Prestidigitation one of the Magic Castle's strangest theatres. Since the space was the former parking structure, there were no choices to accommodate a typical stage setting.

Posters (T1) from the show "It's Magic!" decorate the Parlour of Prestidigitation walls. "It's Magic!" began in 1956 at the Wilshire Ebell Theatre and ran for 20 years as an annual event and then moved to the Variety Arts Theater downtown for another 8 years. After taking a ten year hiatus, "It's Magic!" resurfaced at the Alex Theatre in Glendale in 1994 and is again respected as the most prestigious show in magic. Issued in limited editions, these posters are a rare look at the history of this yearly magic show. Earl Newman was the artist of the poster designs from 1966-1969. Robert LaPlaine hand made each poster from 1970 through 1974.

The smallest portion of the two-tiered chandelier (T2) came from the Los Angeles Real Estate Bureau building at Washington and Hope streets.

The rich mahogany paneling (T3) came from the same church in Whittier as the art glass window in front of the theatre and behind the Palace Bar.

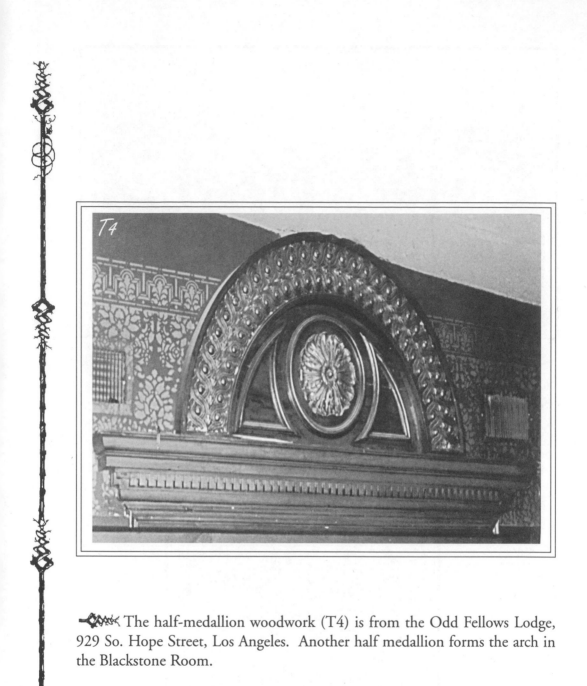

The half-medallion woodwork (T4) is from the Odd Fellows Lodge, 929 So. Hope Street, Los Angeles. Another half medallion forms the arch in the Blackstone Room.

Inner Circle/Ballroom

The Inner Circle/Ballroom is comprised of the Albert Peller Theatre, the Inner Circle Museum, the Grand Ballroom, the William Larsen, Sr. Memorial Library, and the Jack Oakie Memorial Ladies Room. The Inner Circle was constructed as the second phase of the parking structure/theatre project.

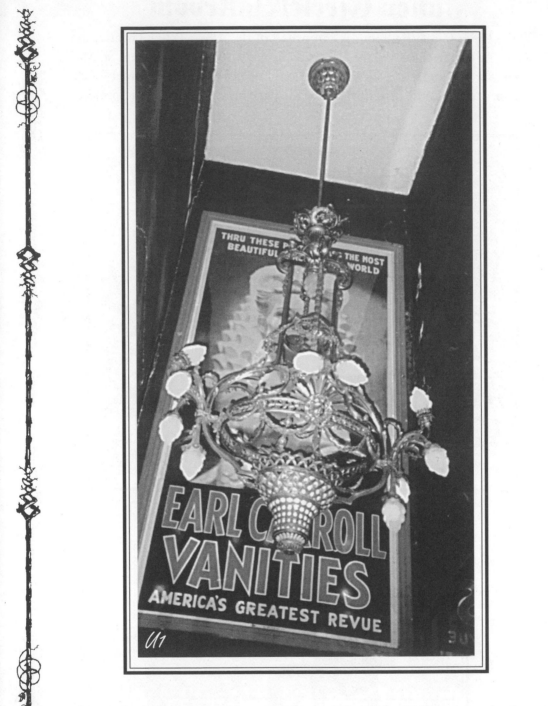

The chandelier (U1) at the base of the stairs leading into the Inner Circle is from England.

The beautiful wrought iron handrail (U2) came from the grand stairway in a magnificent mansion next to the Wilshire Ebell Theatre. The mansion was torn down in 1965 for a parking lot. The wrought iron handrail may be seen in its full majesty in the film "The Happiest Millionaire."

Caricatures (U3) of additional members line the walls leading into the Inner Circle.

A three dimensional reenactment of Harry Kellar's levitation (U4) is prominently displayed in the showcase. T. Nelson Downs (1867-1938) created an act utilizing only coins. His palming coin collection is secured in the display case as you enter the Inner Circle.

Three-sheet posters (U5) advertise magicians like The Great Carter (1874-1936) and Alexander (U6), The Man Who Knows, (1880-1954) as you enter the Inner Circle area. Alexander (1819-1909) aka Herr Alexander learned magic by assisting German magician Ferdinand Becker in 1839.

Edgar Bergen's "Charlie McCarthy" little cocktail bar "stage" (U7) stands at the entrance to the Inner Circle. Charlie's dramatic silhouette captures his charming persona.

A large black box near the entrance to the Inner Circle is "Pepper's Ghost" illusion (U8) created by Member Yale Gracey. This model is the original working exhibit created for Walt Disney's Haunted Mansion at Disneyland. Believe it or not, Yale developed the principle of the illusion totally separate from the magicial effect that dates back about one hundred years.

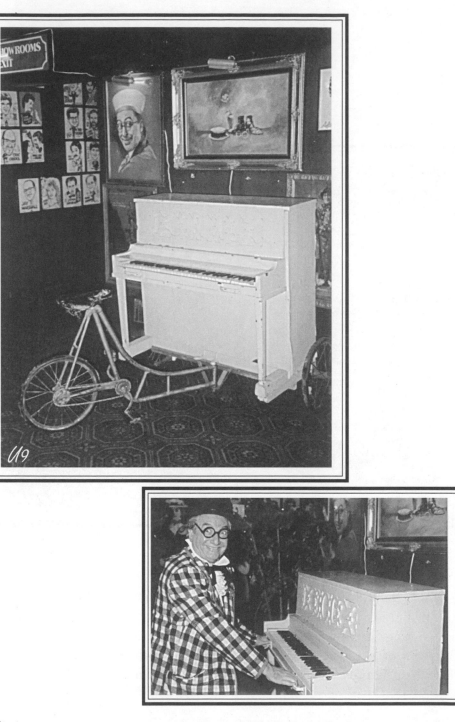

Ed Wynn's piano bike (U9) was one of Wynn's favorite comedy props. The bike, circa 1932, as well as other Ed Wynn memorabilia (U10) was uncovered by his son, Keenan Wynn, in a Bekins storage vault. Milt has been known to give his Ed Wynn impression and has been seen impersonating Mr. Wynn at Halloween.

The 300 lb. iron "Saloon Bar" sign (U11) hung over the entrance to the Granby Arms pub near the Maskelyne & Devant's Egyptian Hall in London. The sign proclaims its title in large gold leaf letters that dates back to the early 1800's.

The oil portrait (U12) of Charlie Earle Miller (1909-1989), world renowned sleight of hand magician, particularly noted for his Cup and Balls and Rice Bowl routines, is featured on the Albert Peller Theatre entrance wall.

U13/U14

The carved arches (U13) of the back portion of the "Hello, Dolly" bar were originally part of a bar in San Francisco that survived the great San Francisco earthquake and fire in 1906, only to be stored for half a century in a loft in Santa Barbara before finding a home at the Magic Castle.

The two art glass windows that adorn the back bar (U14) came from the Granby Arms Pub which was part of the Granby Hotel in London. The Granby was a gathering place for theatre, music and literary types in the 19th century. It was named after John Manners (1638-1711) who was the first Duke of Ruttland and created the Marquis of Granby in 1703.

U15/U16

The large white turned columns (U15) came from Ollie Hammond's Restaurant on LaCienega.

The Hello Dolly Bar (U16) was part of the Harmonia Gardens set for the film, "Hello, Dolly". The bar top used the last of the bird's eye maple flooring from Hollywood High School.

Gene Fowler was a living legend. He was a novelist, biographer, screenwriter, poet, raconteur and wit, and was among the most famous of the talented raffish journalist-writers of the 1920's and 30's. He was a great friend of Damon Runyon, Ring Lardner, Jack Dempsey, W.C. Fields, Red Skelton and Babe Ruth. He was a writer of bestselling novels and such biographies as "Good Night, Sweet Prince" (Barrymore), "Schnozzola" (Durante), and "Beau James" (NY Mayor Walker). Visitors to Fowler's writing den would often leave their hats on his hat rack. This started his collection of celebrity hats (U17). The display cases were designed by John Shrum (of course) and contain the authentic hats of stars and famous people who were known for their hats: Jimmy Durante's crushed fedora, a top hat worn by Mayor Jimmy Walker, an elaborate plumed Hedda Hopper hat, and Milt's favorite W.C. Fields hat that W.C. wore to John Barrymore's funeral (U18). (In those days, everyone wore black to a funeral but Fields hated black. He rode in a white limousine when the traditional limos were black. The hat he wore to the funeral is indeed black but W.C. inserted a colorful feather in its hat band as a gesture of defiance to the establishment. Barrymore would have liked that.)

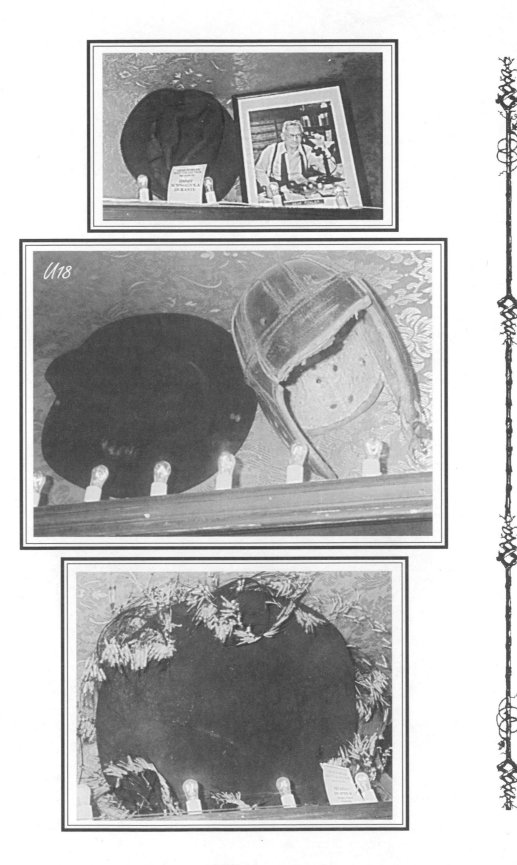

The Albert Peller Theatre

Albert Peller (1910-1989) was an amateur magician and attorney who loved the Magic Castle. When he passed away, his benevolent widow, Triny Peller, also an accomplished magician, donated the financing to create the Albert Peller Theatre used for impromptu magic performances, private parties, screenings, and as a video/film viewing room. It was dedicated as the Albert Peller Theatre on February 2, 1997.

The portrait of Albert Peller (U18)was commissioned by his widow, Triny.

Here, in the interior of the theatre, we find more tin ceiling (U19) from the downtown fire house station.

Inside the Albert Peller Theatre, along the back walls, are what used to be the ceiling beams (U20) of Berkeley Square on Western and Adams.

Six MGM lights (U21) were purchased at the MGM auction that closed the studio facility in Culver City in 1970, four of which reside here in the Peller Theatre.

One of the posters decorating the Albert Peller Theatre walls is of T. Nelson Downs (1867-1938), who billed himself as the King of Koins (U22). His ability to produce coins from the air was phenomenal.

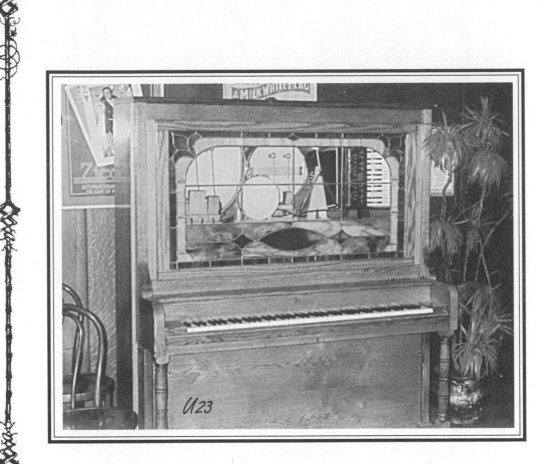

The nickelodeon piano "Invisible Izzy" (U23) was donated by Member Producer Bob Stivers ("Circus of the Stars") and his wife, Bunny.

On loan from Ozzi Malini is a display of Polish born Max Malini's (U24) (1873-1942) artifacts and costumes. Malini's trademark effect was a production of a large object, such as a 4x4 block of ice, from under a borrowed hat. He was a favorite of the rich and famous.

Outside the Albert Peller Theatre are several display cases (U25). These displays change constantly and have shown tributes to Robert Hays, Spike Jones, and may have some of the following: On loan from the SPVA, Society for the Preservation of Variety Arts, are artifacts including Paul Winchell's "Jerry Mahoney," Jack Shafton's "Cowgirl" and the "Horse," "Jimmy Durante" marionette and Emmett Kelly marionettes created by Verne Langdon. Nicknamed "Merry Dolls" these marionettes brought smiles to many a face.

Edgar Bergen (U26) was a devoted magician who considered ventriloquism as "the art of illusion." He created three characters: Charlie McCarthy, Mortimer Snerd and Effie Klinker. Edgar died on stage in Las Vegas in 1978 at the age of 75. His wife was the well known actress Frances Bergen and their daughter is one of TV's best known stars, Candice Bergen.

Mrs. Francis Bergen donated the fascinating Bergen memorabilia (U27) to the Magic Castle, including custom hats worn by Edgar's co-stars and a rare Petrie Lewis "Rose Bush" which was one of Edgar's favorite effects in magic.

The "Jimmy Durante" Personality Marionette (U28) was created for TV's "The Jimmy Durante Show" and was later employed in the Shafton's highly acclaimed night club act.

Outside the Albert Peller Theatre, above the Grand Ballroom, are square mirrored panels that give an illusion of an endless, mystical ceiling (U29).

A very nice lady who lived in Watts had heard about the legendary Milt and his salvaging quests. She called the Magic Castle and offered several art glass windows, if he were interested. Inundated with art glass windows at the time, Milt never connected with her. A mere seven years later she called again. She informed Milt that she was demolishing the buildings to make way for a mini-mall and that the glass windows would be destroyed if he didn't want them. Milt canceled an important meeting and quickly drove to Watts. When he got there, the windows were so dirty Milt could not appreciate them for their antique beauty but he purchased them anyway. When he got the windows back to the Magic Castle and cleaned them, he found designs of a castle, food, and music! These windows now are the art glass wall (U30) for the Grand Ballroom.

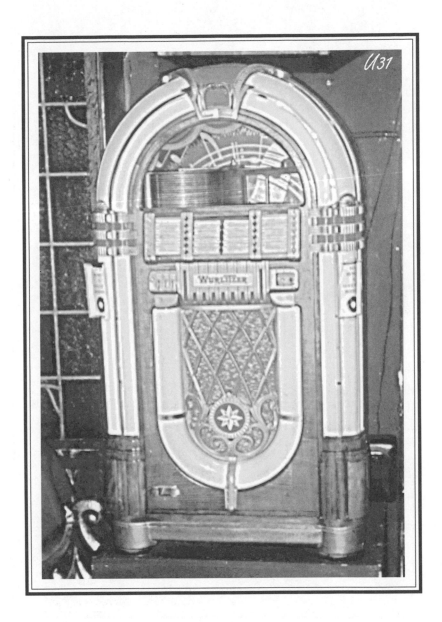

The 1050 Wurlitzer jukebox (U31), circa 1940 was a prop used in Milt's production of the Sherman Brothers musical "Victory Canteen" at the Ivar Theatre in 1971.

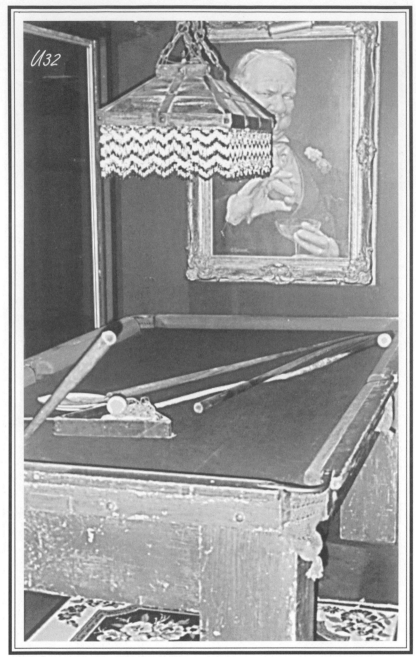

Please don't disturb the ghost of W.C. who is probably setting up his next shot on the W.C. Fields' trick billiard ball table (U32). The table is on permanent loan to the SPVA/Castle by the Fields' estate. Note the cue stick that probably gave W.C. his advantage over other players. You might even hear him mutter, "Seems to be slightly warped."

The oil portrait of W.C. (U33) is by artist Member Carl Babcock.

Madame Carnak is a fantastic and very rare turn-of-the-century wax figure fortune-telling automaton (U34) that dispenses comic predictions typical of the Johnny Carson character on "The Tonight Show." Johnny used the figure on the show and John Shrum got the NBC Special Effects craftsmen to restore it for the Magic Castle.

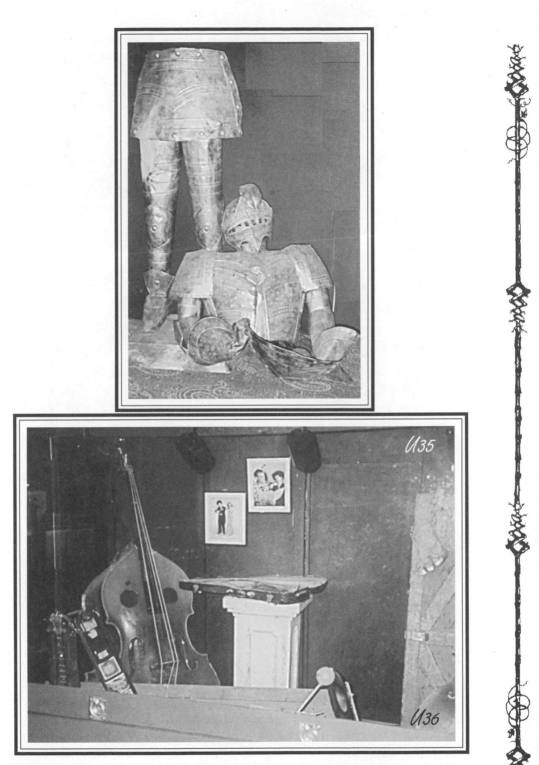

On occasion you might find Spike's Jones' display of his instruments and other memorabilia (U35) which depend entirely on Milt's whim.

NBC scenic artist A. Obregon replaced the Napoleonic officer's face with that of Milt's in the large portrait (U36) outside the library entrance.

U37/U38

~CANK A new addition to the Magic Castle is the Classroom (U37) where classes are taught by magicians and professors alike.

~CANK "The Dancing Master" (U38) is the current "movie" in the rare, antique coin operated Mutoscope. It is valued at $6,000 to $8,000!

William W. Larsen
Memorial Library

Hidden from public view, reserved exclusively for members of the Academy of Magical Arts, one can find the William W. Larsen Memorial Library dedicated to the memories of William Larsen, Sr. and William Larsen, Jr. This library is one of the largest working libraries dedicated to magic and the allied arts in the world of magic as well as the largest theatrical research area on the West Coast.

Currently there are over 4,000 columns of books, 2,500 hours of videos, and the number of resources available to members grows daily. The collection includes rare books that date back to 1769 plus complete editions of magical periodicals from around the world. Additionally, the library contains many very valuable books signed by authors, including five first edition volumes personally inscribed by Harry Houdini.

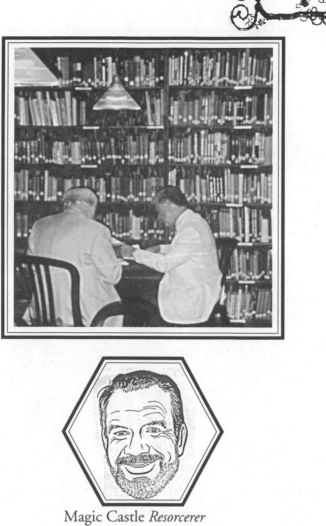

Magic Castle *Resorcerer*
and affable librarian.
Hal Hale

𝔄lso in the collection is a complete set of the famous Goldston "Locked Books" published in the late 1800's. To protect the secrets in these books, the publisher had a lock mounted into each corner.

𝔗he library is a member of the Southern California Answer Network, a research facility that is used by television and motion picture studios in doing research for individual projects.

𝔗he video library includes over 2,500 hours of magicians performing and lecturing as well as Magic Castle Awards and "It's Magic!" shows, instructional tapes and current motion picture and television shows that feature magicians, including rare footage of Harry Houdini and Dante in both public and private motion pictures.

The Gothic arched art glass window (V1) in the library came from the Phillips mansion on Crescent Drive in Beverly Hills (Phillips as in oil as opposed to Milk of Magnesia) and is another item rescued by Ernie Evans. You may notice the art glass border does not continue around the bottom.

The window was mounted on a grand staircase above a marble table. Milt surmises the workers simply eliminated the bottom panel to make the window fit the space. That bottom panel didn't mean much in 1910 but it probably had one little thing: a signature LCT [Louis Comfort Tiffany (1848-1933)] at the right hand bottom corner. The window is most likely an original and genuine Tiffany museum-quality piece. The difference in value between a signed and unsigned Tiffany amounts to something in the six figure range. Members David E. Green, Jean Cantor and Ruth Bartling donated funds to have the window repaired before its installation in the library area.

Oil portrait of William Larsen, Sr. (V2) was painted by Geri Larsen in the 1960's.

Geri Larsen's portrait (V3) was painted by the late Joel Makray, a world famous artist and a Santa Barbaran friend and neighbor, in 1985.

One of the most unique and rare magic programs at the Magic Castle is a silk program (V4) that commemorates the command performance of Italian Signor Bosco (1793-1863) for Queen Victoria, September 1855. Billy McComb noted that the only silk program bordered with Honiton lace was the one given to the Queen. Thus this was Queen Victoria's own personal program for the evening. Milt purchased it sight unseen for a mere pittance. Balmoral Castle was the royal residence for Queen Victoria when in Scotland. Bosco spoke and performed in eleven different languages. The program offers an evening of magic and ventriloquism and includes "The Astonishing Snuff Box."

Dating back to 1870 is an automaton conjurer (V5) in a period costume that performs a version of "The Cups & Balls" illusion. It was donated by Canadian magician Sam Cramer from Montreal.

Also on display is a rare statue entitled "The Traveling Magician." The piece is a cast sculpture (V6) dating back to 1877, created by famed American artist John Rogers, who is best known for his statuette groupings. This was donated by Jack Swimmer, internationally famous magician and mentalist, who was President of the Academy of Magical Arts & Sciences (the original organization which later was resurrected to become today's Academy of Magical Arts). The piece was presented to Mr. Swimmer by the Chavez College of Magic as an Achievement Award in the field of magic.

In a display case (V7) are more rare magic props from the collection of Simon Ortega that includes a rare Houlette, steamboat playing cards, a Thayer Passe-Passe bottle; Rice Bowl, Flags of All Nations, Changing Bag, Crystal Casket and the Appearing Bird.

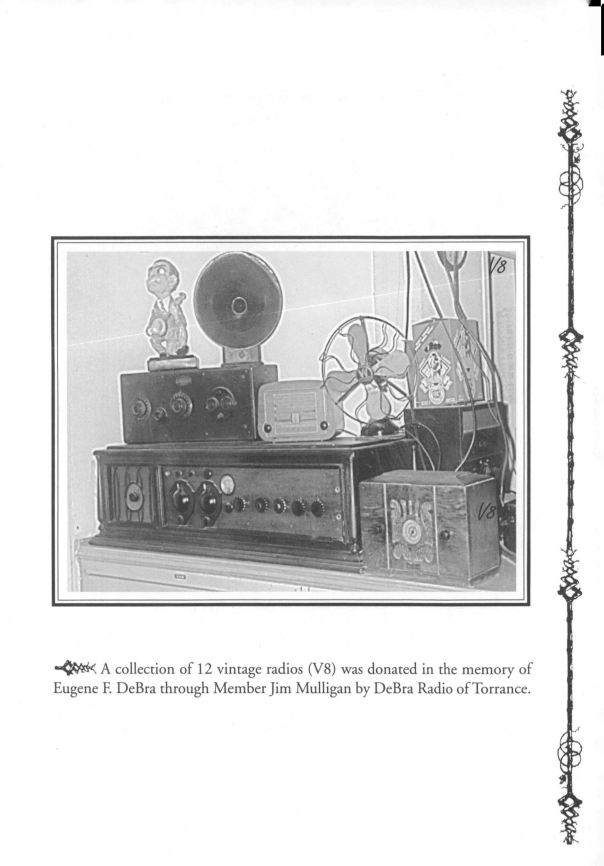

A collection of 12 vintage radios (V8) was donated in the memory of Eugene F. DeBra through Member Jim Mulligan by DeBra Radio of Torrance.

A signed 1846 etching (V9) by Gedr. B.J. Rauh, of Austrian born Johann Hofzinser (1806-1875), was donated to the Magic Castle in 1993 by Magischeklubwien. Hofzinser created many effects and prepared cards and was possibly the inventor of the clock dial.

David Devant (1868-1941) was considered one of Britain's greatest magicians. He performed at the world famous Egyptian Hall in London for over a decade and debuted his invention of the "Artist's Dream" where a painting of a woman came alive. A greeting card with a 1940 postmark (V10) from Devant to Servais LeRoy and a dramatic hand flyer (by arrangement with Maskelyne & Devant) are framed artifacts in the library.

William W. Larsen, Sr.
(1904-1953)

William Larsen, Sr. was born in Greenbay, Wisconsin on December 31, 1905, just before midnight. He often joked that he was quite a few years older before he realized that all the fuss made at midnight on December 31st was not in honor of his birthday. After going to school in Wisconsin, he came to California in 1922, to attend Occidental College. He went on to the University of Southern California Law School and passed the bar, going into private practice as an attorney.

Mr. Larsen met Geraldine Conrad at Occidental College and they were married in 1925. They had two sons, William, Jr. born in 1928 and Milton, born in 1931. That became the Larsen Family, which was better known to the world as "Magic's First Family of Magicians." While his practice in criminal law took most of his attention, Mr. Larsen always found time for his magic. He had a partner, T. Page Wright, and together they published their first original effect in the magicians' magazine, "Sphinx," in August of 1920. The effect was their version of the famous rising card trick. Their friendship continued until Mr. Wright was tragically killed in an automobile accident.

Bill continued to create a vast amount of original magical material throughout his lifetime. One book of his writings has been published, although it will require two more volumes to complete everything that he ever wrote for magicians.

In 1936 Bill started his own magazine, "Genii" He was assisted by his wife, Geri, and they successfully published the periodical until 1953. After that, it was continued by Geri and their son, Bill. After Bill, Jr's death, his wife Irene now publishes the magazine and it is edited by Bill's youngest daughter Erika. Genii Magazine celebrated its sixtieth anniversary in 1996.

While Mr. Larsen's law practice was his chief source of income, the Larsen Family did take a year off in 1939 to tour the United States with a full evening magic show. They did not play in theatres, but they performed for men's clubs, women's clubs, resort hotels and other smaller venues. During this time, Geri performed in about one-third of the program and the boys, Bill and Milt, dressed in "Phillip Morris" bellboy-type jackets, acted as the assistants.

In 1945, William Larsen, Sr. decided to take a rest from the criminal law business, to devote full time to magic. He purchased the Thayer Magical Manufacturing Company, which was founded by Floyd Thayer in 1907. As part of the exchange, the Larsen house in Pasadena went to the Thayer's, while the Thayer house in Los Angeles became home to the Larsen Family. Irene still lives in the house which is named "Brookledge," after the small brook that runs through the property. The house also contains a full-size theatre and tropical gardens. Almost every famous magician from the 1940's to the present day has visited the house and dined with the Larsen family.

William Larsen Sr. died on July 5, 1953, at the age of only 48. It then became the goal of his sons, Bill, Jr. and Milt to carry on with his dream of a private club for magicians. Although he was never able to see the dream fulfilled during his lifetime, we know that somewhere, somehow, he realizes the success that his vision inspired.

W1

W2

━━◆━━ In the Jack Oakie Memorial Ladies Room in the Inner Circle Jack Oakie memorabilia (W1), photos and other paraphernalia cover the walls. Jack Oakie was a very active member of the Castle. His wife contributed funding to build the rest room facilities in the Inner Circle and thought Jack would be amused to have the Ladies Room named in his honor. Obviously the great comedian had a wonderful sense of humor.

━━◆━━ An old Stromberg-Carlsen radio (W2) and a beautiful carved wood and velvet settee create the lounge area. From time to time you will even hear old Jack Oakie radio shows on this strange radio of the past.

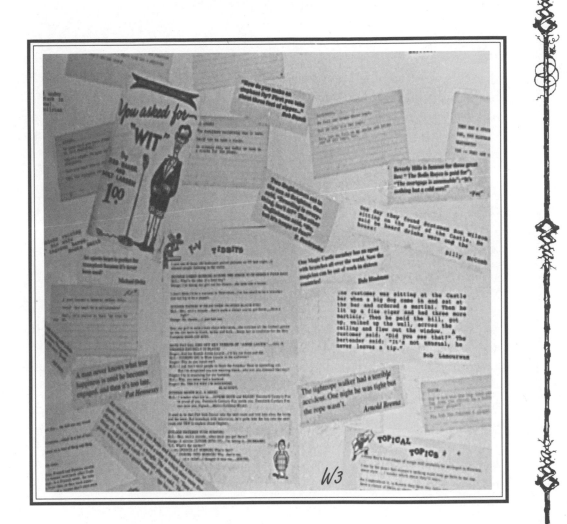

Every joke (W3) you have ever heard in Vaudeville shows of the past comprise the wallpaper of the men's room.

Afterword

The Magic Castle has always intrigued me. After I became a member, I had an even greater opportunity to study the architecture, decor and elements that comprise the old Victorian mansion in the Hollywood Hills. When Milt began his personal tours of the Magic Castle, I jumped at the chance each and every month to satisfy my curiosity. What started out as an unquenchable thirst for more information about the physical building quickly escalated into a full-time devotion.

I delighted in uncovering some old and obscure photograph of the Lane Mansion or what the Magic Castle looked like in the early days with the zolotone effect. My attempt was to capture and document the enchanting interior and preserve the history of the combined elements that make the Magic Castle the Magic Castle... sprinkling a little magic history and facts along the way.

My journey was not without frustration. Not only is the interior of the Magic Castle dark and dramatically lit, but lights reflected off most surfaces I attempted to photograph. However, eighty percent of the photographs shown within this book were, indeed, taken during one of the numerous tours I took with Milt. These photos were augmented by historical photographs, a few time lapse photos for the most difficult of subjects by Ron Jackson, and photographs that I came upon on Milt's office as I was working on the book. It would be nice to acknowledge all the photographers who have contributed to this book but its impossible to trace their origin. Whoever you are, thank-you.

My next frustration came in trying to overcome my ignorance in desktop publishing on a Macintosh with a mind of its own (and a disappearing hard drive that magically reappeared at will), so I recruited a computer guru and friend that helped me get through all the enigmas that usually reared their ugly heads at least once a week.

It's been a rewarding, tremendously fulfilling and creative experience for me in spite of the fact that Milt seemed to delight in announcing to me the next time I saw him that he had changed something else. Or when I found that I had notes with conflicting information, Milt would reply, "Well, which version do you like?" Obviously, I tried to be as accurate as possible within my given limitations.

I hope that I was successful in my portrayal of this fascinating establishment and that you enjoy the experience in learning about this seductive and charming castle. I know I did!

I'm also very proud to add: **Mi castle es su castle!**

... to be continued...